SPIRITUAL MODALITIES

D1714581

SPIRITUAL MODALITIES

PRAYER AS RHETORIC AND PERFORMANCE

WILLIAM FITZGERALD

THE PENNSYLVANIA STATE UNIVERSITY PRESS
UNIVERSITY PARK, PENNSYLVANIA

Library of Congress Cataloging-in-Publication Data

FitzGerald, William, 1961–
Spiritual modalities : prayer as rhetoric and performance / William FitzGerald.
        p.   cm.
Includes bibliographical references and index.
Summary: "Explores prayer as a rhetorical art, examining situations, strategies, and
performative modes of discourse directed to the divine"—Provided by publisher.
ISBN 978-0-271-05622-7 (cloth : alk. paper)
ISBN 978-0-271-05623-4 (pbk. : alk. paper)
1. Prayer.
2. Rhetoric.
3. Performance.
I. Title.

BL560.F58   2012
204'.3—dc23
2012017711

FOR *Thomas and Elizabeth*

Contents

ACKNOWLEDGMENTS / viii
LIST OF ABBREVIATIONS / x

Introduction: Prayer:
The Rediscovered Country / 1

1
Prayer and Its Situations:
Meditation on *Kairos* and *Krisis* / 11

2
"Hear Us, O Lord":
Audience and Address in Communicating with the Divine / 31

3
Invocations of Spirit:
Prayer as Speech Act / 52

4
The Dance of Attitude:
Prayer as the Performance of Reverence / 71

5
Performing the Memorare:
Prayer as a Rhetorical Art of Memory / 100

6
Bodies and Spirits in Virtual Motion:
Prayer and Delivery in Cyberspace / 115

Conclusion: Does Rhetoric Have a Prayer? / 131

NOTES / 139
WORKS CITED / 145
INDEX / 153

Acknowledgments

I remember distinctly when, over lunch at the University of Maryland too long ago, Jeanne Fahnestock offered the rhetoric of prayer as an estimable project someone ought to take up. Although it would be some time before I concluded that the prayer project was mine, I remain grateful to Jeanne for her suggestion then and, far more so, for her wise counsel and encouragement in the years since.

When I did take up prayer as the subject of my research, it was under the inspired direction of Mark Turner, who gave me latitude to explore prayer's cognitive underpinnings, particularly in ways attentive to the poetics of belief and ritual. What ability I have to discuss spiritual matters with sympathetic detachment I owe to time spent with Mark on the figurative dimensions of discourse directed toward divine beings as suitable objects of address. Among many things, prayer is a profound encounter with the workings of mind and language. I happily acknowledge Mark's guidance in pursuing this insight, albeit in identifiably rhetorical idioms here, especially those of Kenneth Burke.

I owe much to my fine mentors at the University of Maryland, College Park, John Schilb and David Wyatt, and to Shirley Wilson Logan, Marie Boor Tonn, and Michael Marcuse, who, as readers of an early version of this book, offered much food for thought. I owe an unpayable debt to Michael Marcuse for his deep insights into the implicit promise of my effort to bridge secular and sacred rhetoric and for his unwavering personal support. And I am especially grateful to my graduate colleague in rhetoric and composition at Maryland Todd Oakley for his sagacity in helping me articulate a rhetoric of prayer.

I thank former colleagues at the University of Maryland, Baltimore County (UMBC), in particular Christoph Irmscher and Lucille McCarthy, for their guidance and encouragement, and my current colleagues at Rutgers University Camden, in particular Chris Fitter, Rafey Habib, Carol Singley, and Howard Marchitello, for their phenomenal support and for generously reading a work in progress. I also thank colleagues Ellen Ledoux, Keith Green, and Wojtek Wolfe for their astute contributions to portions of this book. And I give special thanks to secretary and confidante Dee Jonczak.

Spiritual Modalities benefits from many opportunities to present work in progress at academic conferences. I thank Patrick Shaw and Dana Anderson, fellow travelers along the rhetorical road that intersects with religion. I thank editors Jack Selzer and Bob Weiss for their insights in developing a paper on *prayer* as a key term in Burkean rhetoric, later published in *Kenneth Burke and His Circles*. In 2007, I was privileged to host a Rhetoric Society of America Institute workshop on rhetoric and religion; in 2009, I attended a similar workshop led by Robert Glenn Howard and Susan Zaeske. I warmly thank participants of both workshops, in particular Ben Crosby, Michael de Palma, James Webber, and Kari Tremeryn, for their helpful advice. I am indebted to Martin Camper, Heather Brown, Beth Allen, and Dahira Binford for their generous reading of multiple chapters. Any credit for stylistic virtues goes to them.

The editorial staff of Penn State University Press have been beyond supportive throughout the publication process. I express my profound debt to Kendra Boileau for recognizing the promise in my project, to my anonymous readers, whose recommendations were invaluable, and to copy editor Jeffrey Lockridge for his unerring good sense and sympathetic reading of my text. All credit for the title *Spiritual Modalities* is owed my friend and colleague Jonathan Buehl; in that one gift among many, Jonathan helped me realize a broader vision for my book. His support at every stage for several years is beyond words or thanks.

And, finally, to my wife, Emilia, and daughter, Magdalena, for believing in me and allowing me to finish "Daddy's book," and to my mother, Elizabeth, my father, Thomas (of blessed memory), and all in my family, I offer a deep prayer of thanksgiving.

Abbreviations

Because the corpus of Kenneth Burke looms large in this account, I have abbreviated the titles of his works parenthetically cited in the text and notes.

ATH	Attitudes Toward History
GM	A Grammar of Motives
LASA	Language as Symbolic Action
PC	Permanence and Change.
PLF	Philosophy of Literary Form
RM	A Rhetoric of Motives

Most of my biblical quotations are taken from the New Revised Standard Version; those from other versions are identified by the following abbreviations:

ELLC	English Language Liturgical Consultation version
NAB	New American Bible
NIV	New International Version
NKJV	New King James Version

INTRODUCTION
PRAYER:
THE REDISCOVERED COUNTRY

> However badly needed a good book on prayer is, I shall never try
> to write it. . . . In a book one would inevitably seem to
> be attempting, not discussion, but instruction.
>
> —C. S. Lewis, *Letters to Malcolm: Chiefly on Prayer*

The phenomenal rise in demand for books and merchandise devoted to religion or spirituality over the past twenty years has not been confined to specialty stores or niche markets. Spirituality is big business. Indeed, books on "soul care" regularly top best-seller lists, and websites devoted to religion proliferate as our digital roots deepen. Noteworthy in this development was the 2000 publication of Bruce Wilkinson's *The Prayer of Jabez*—its subject a text obscurely lodged in the Bible's first book of Chronicles: "Jabez was more honorable than his brothers. His mother had named him Jabez, saying, 'I gave birth to him in pain.' Jabez cried out to the God of Israel, 'Oh, that you would bless me and enlarge my territory! Let your hand be with me, and keep me from harm so that I will be free from pain.' And God granted his request" (4:9–10, NIV). Wilkinson claims this prayer holds "the key to a life of extraordinary favor from God" (8). Many were curious whether this claim had merit. Indeed, evangelization on behalf of the prayer resulted in sales of more than ten million copies. Its success spawned spin-offs in deluxe and teen editions, study guides, and paraphernalia (key chains, wall plaques, coffee mugs, and so on). The prayer's "message" about God enlarging one's territory resonated with many at a time when a gospel of prosperity had gained currency in evangelical circles.

Wilkinson sees in this neglected prayer a tool for unlocking material blessings: "I challenge you to make the Jabez prayer for blessing part of the daily fabric of your life. To do that, I encourage you to follow unwaveringly the plan outlined here for the next thirty days. By the end of that time, you'll be noticing significant changes in your life, and the prayer will be on its way to becoming a treasured, lifelong habit" (86). Although fueled by a potent blend of method and hucksterism, Wilkinson's exhortations are squarely in a familiar framework, where prayer functions as a strategy for meeting spiritual and material needs. The underlying message of both the biblical text and Wilkinson's *The Prayer of Jabez* is simple: God grants requests appropriately performed. Both reflect a widespread belief in the rhetorical power of prayer—that divine beings can be appealed to with profit.

The Prayer of Jabez appeared soon after I began the project that would become *Spiritual Modalities*. At the time, a project on prayer and rhetoric seemed on the fringes of respectability in scholarly circles. *The Prayer of Jabez* provided evidence both for and against this established judgment. I recall being struck by its naive reductionism: recite *this* prayer, *this* way, to *these* effects. Yet here was a text sparking keen interest in prayer, even though many readers questioned its facile pronouncements in favor of more nuanced perspectives on prayer's presumed efficacy.

About a year later, the events of September 11 would usher in more sober perspectives on prayer's power and limitations, uses and abuses. With the dawn of a new millennium came the realization that religion would not readily yield to secularism. If anything, religion seems more relevant in an anxious age of clashing cultures and profound uncertainty. And prayer, as a signature expression of religion, seems less an artifact of a particular culture or era, something to be outgrown or overcome, perhaps, than a practice fundamental to our condition as beings blessed, or cursed, with language.

This is the insight that informs this book. Prayer is a discursive art in which capacities central to our human experience with language come together with respect to supersensory, superordinate, supernatural reality, typically imagined in the form of culturally significant otherworldly audiences—divine beings with whom human beings enjoy rich, complex relationships. However grand or modest the claims made about it, prayer is notoriously difficult to delimit. Efforts to do so tend to wall off prayer to the neglect of its porous relations with other discourse.

Spiritual Modalities explores these relations using rhetoric as an interpretive lens. In doing so, it responds to a growing call to articulate the intersection of rhetoric and religion. As early as 1961, in *The Rhetoric of Religion*, Kenneth Burke asserted that "the study of religion falls under the heading of *rhetoric* in the sense that rhetoric is the art of *persuasion*, and religious cosmogonies are designed, in the last analysis, as exceptionally thoroughgoing modes of persua-sion" (v, emphasis in original). In 2000, Walter Jost and Wendy Olmsted moti-vated a groundbreaking anthology, *Rhetorical Invention and Religious Inquiry*, by asking, "Are rhetoric and religion in some sense 'essentially' wedded?" They responded that "when firmly placed within religious, social, and intellectual history or located within the study of theology, the convergence of rhetoric and religion takes one to the most central issues of several fields—philosophy, psy-chology, literary history, and art—interpreting relations between self, language, and world that are central to past and present cultures as well as to their forms of life" (2). And, at the 2005 biennial meeting of the International Society for the History of Rhetoric (ISHR), President Laurent Pernot called for a substantial reengagement with religion in rhetorical studies, identifying prayer and hymn as modes of discourse demanding particular attention.[1] By this time, a turn to religion was evident in rhetorical scholarship addressing theology, preaching, and the place of religious discourse in the public sphere.[2]

But, even though inquiry at the intersection of rhetoric and religion con-tinues to advance, prayer has yet to be substantively engaged. Indeed, so thor-oughly rhetorical is prayer it hardly seems in need of interrogation as such. Specific prayers or genres of prayer may invite interpretation as texts, yes, but prayer as a mode of discourse? In addition, prayer resists theorization not ulti-mately directed toward practice. Finally, problems of scope and method arise in moving beyond the analysis of specific texts to more general claims about prayer as rhetorical action. Prayer is decidedly not a monolith. Whose prayer, then, to study? What genres and what performative modes?

As the first systematic study of prayer in relation to rhetoric, *Spiritual Modal-ities* addresses a deficit to advance a deeper understanding of both. It exam-ines prayer as a "rediscovered country"—a locale at once strange and familiar. The best guidebooks succeed in both familiarizing and defamiliarizing their subjects. With this in mind, *Spiritual Modalities* presents prayer in language distinct from a religious idiom, yet sympathetic to prayer's abiding religious concerns and to claims made on its behalf. That language is rhetoric.

In *The Varieties of Religious Experience*, William James characterizes prayer as "the very soul and essence of religion" (464). The philosopher Emmanuel Levinas maintains that prayer is tasked with nothing less than "repairing the ruins of creation" ("Prayer Without Demand" 233). Finally, Kenneth Burke pro-poses that "the man who does not pray cannot build his character" (*ATH* 322). Such earnest pronouncements invite speculation about prayer's situations and strategies, modes and motivations. If, in the elegant formulation of Saint John Damascene, prayer is "a raising of the heart and mind to God," how might this insight be understood in discourse less theologically motivated? I read the present moment as opportune to rediscover the power, richness, and sophistication of prayer as discourse. Rhetoric—the "architectonic art"—can and must flex its theoretical muscles to respond to prayer more robustly than it has (McKeon 201). Yet how best to proceed in an effort of rediscovery?

Rediscovering Prayer as Spiritual Modalities

Prayer can be located in many places—*etymologically* in petition and praise, *psychologically* in the individual soul, *sociologically* in the practice of a society, *anthropologically* in the expression of a culture, and even *economically* in the accounting and exchanges of commerce. Finally, prayer can be located *essentially* in some purity of act or state of mind in relation to divine beings. All such efforts divide prayer from other discourse and distinguish this kind of prayer from that. In contrast, a *rhetorical* approach to prayer encompasses all these locations or orientations, taking as its chief orientation what human actors do in performing prayer and the interpretive frames that inform that performance.

Spiritual Modalities is not a work of cultural or intellectual history. It advances no claims about prayer's development in theoretical or practical terms. Nor does it establish a narrative about the place of prayer within rhetorical studies or about rhetoric's role in prayer as a formal compositional art. Rather, as a sympathetic application of methods to materials, it articulates rhetorical principles operating in prayer, particularly insofar as prayer exemplifies these principles.

To bring prayer and rhetoric into relation, there are few better places to begin than with a burnt offering before a deity—"communication" at its most elemental. In the book of Genesis, brothers Cain and Abel perform such sacrifices (4:1–16). For reasons unexplained, Abel's animal sacrifice pleases the Lord, whereas Cain's plant sacrifice does not. Soon after, Cain slays Abel in the fields from which Cain has gathered his offering. Whether the attitude that leads to this first fratricide is cause or consequence of Cain's sacrifice being rejected is left unclear. But the implication is clear: words and deeds communicate an essential attitude of their performers. Something is amiss with Cain's attitude and therefore with his act of sacrifice—it constitutes "bad rhetoric." In juxtaposing these instances of successful and failed rhetoric, this Bible story implicitly recognizes prayer through sacrifice as a performance of attitude through acts of communication. The proper attitude for prayer can be characterized as "piety." This account argues for *reverence* as a fitting term to describe prayer's pious orientation toward someone or something as manifested in socially constitutive communicative acts.

Prayer is par excellence a performance of attitude—at once interior and exterior, a matter of soul and of body. The production and circulation of discourse is likewise central to prayer. Prayer occurs in social networks linking performers communally across time and space. Though localized in individual bodies, prayer is not only personal but also social. Individual prayer is authorized and sponsored by communities of practice. Its abstract, meta-rhetorical character permits its easy migration into new sites of performance.

In simplest terms, prayer can be described as "talking to God (or some other divine being)." To go beyond these terms, it is necessary to describe the forms such "talk" may take and the motivations that inspire this activity. Enter rhetoric.

A practical rhetoric of prayer would appropriately emphasize prayer's genres and their enabling assumptions to encourage certain kinds of performance and discourage others. Indeed, there is no shortage of such practical rhetorics in the form of devotional handbooks and model texts. As a *critical* and also *secular* rhetoric, however, *Spiritual Modalities* articulates principles governing prayer in terms that may be alien to the practice and understanding of the discourse communities it examines. The risk in such efforts, of course, is getting important things wrong. The reward is seeing things not fully visible from inside and thus making connections across domains of practice regarded as distinct.

The relationship between prayer and rhetoric can be understood in two basic ways. On the one hand, prayer is a part of rhetoric, a particular use of language for thoroughly persuasive ends; it extends practices of communication among human beings to communication between human and divine beings. In this regard, praise or petition directed toward divine audiences is generated from rhetoric similar to that directed toward human audiences. On the other hand, regarded as especially sincere and soul-searching language, prayer serves as a *counter* to rhetoric, perceived as insincere or self-serving speech. In this sense, prayer is a vital, arguably necessary, proving ground for a more perfect rhetoric. Indeed, one can go so far as to claim no other discourse realizes ideal communication more than authentic acts of prayer.

Even though it can be seen as a resource for elevating discourse, efforts to distance prayer from rhetoric, or to oppose them altogether, are counterproductive.

Conceived as *sacred* discourse, set apart from the ordinary by association with the transcendent, prayer has acquired a counter-rhetorical cast, much as scientific discourse is viewed in certain quarters as rhetoric's other. It is not that prayer goes unrecognized as persuasive language. It is that prayer aspires to ascend the ladder of language to discover a purer language, a rhetoric *beyond* rhetoric, even transcending language altogether to achieve a state of perfect, wordless communion between human and divine beings. This impulse toward rhetorical purity challenges the inherently mixed motives that mark, or mar, discourse.

By contrast, a less pure perspective sees in rhetoric a foundation for *all* symbolic arts. I submit that this perspective, which fails to respect boundaries some would establish for prayer *or* rhetoric, offers the greatest potential for understanding prayer's discursive nature. It sees prayer not as exceptional discourse set apart from or even opposed to ordinary language, but as rhetoric distilled and abstracted to allow for its application in extraordinary contexts. It designates core functions of discourse that make communication possible, and it acknowledges the impulse toward purity and perfection in prayer. Indeed, "prayer" is a name assigned to practices of a better rhetoric.

This perspective negotiates between prayer as ultimate source and ultimate destination of ordinary rhetoric. It places prayer at the center of things people do with language, rather than on the periphery. For prayer is concerned precisely with our capacities to engage other beings in communion and communication, seeking their cooperation through instruments of language. As address to divine beings, prayer abstracts and amplifies aspects of discourse constitutive of all communication. *Spiritual Modalities* recognizes prayer as a cognitive, social, and material practice by which human beings locate themselves (by a *de*fining and *re*fining of motive) in relation to the divine. As discourse addressed to divine beings, prayer is designed to work out our human character and condition as beings at once "languaged" and embodied. Often highly specific in its ends, prayer is concerned with the well-being of persons and communities in relation to the divine, perceived as significantly invested in that well-being.

For a rhetoric of prayer, Kenneth Burke's theory of *dramatism*, introduced in *A Grammar of Motives*, offers a particularly robust framework. Indeed, Burke's pentad of motives (*act, scene, agent, agency,* and *purpose*)—later to include a sixth motive, *attitude*—seems specially designed to articulate prayer's rhetorical character. Centered in action, these motives provide headings for reading cultural artifacts (texts, philosophies, political systems) by which phenomenal complexities are reduced to more manageable terms. Used regularly, a motive becomes an ism, an ideological foregrounding of one motive above others. As Burke observes in *Permanence and Change*, "motives are shorthand terms for situations" (29). At any moment, a single motive such as "scene" or "agent" may serve as key term (or interpretive lens) in a theory of motivation.

Applied to prayer, Burke's motivational grammar reveals discourse addressed to divine beings to be positively brimming with motives. Inherently dramatic, prayer can be read as staged performance in multiple settings, involving complex dynamics of audience and purpose and relying on a wide range of verbal and material instruments to structure its communicative events. Burkean dramatism offers six *pure* motives and as many as sixty *mixed* motives in the form of dramatistic relations ("ratios," e.g., act-scene, scene-act, agent-purpose) to serve as interpretive frames for reading and performing specific prayers and prayer in general. Each avenue of approach selects certain aspects of the whole to emphasize. These approaches structure how prayer is understood and performed.

Spiritual Modalities reads prayer through the three primary motives of scene, act, and attitude. These motives bring out dimensions particular to prayer, yet also fundamental to discourse in the broadest sense. Here I propose that prayer fuses distinct, though interrelated, elements of discursive performance expressible as a "scene of address," an "act of invocation," and an "attitude of reverence." Although one can characterize prayer as "address," "invocation," and "reverence" without relying on Burkean terms, Burke's dramatism offers a systematic, nontheological framework for what those who pray do with language.

Most theological accounts of prayer are principally invested in the motives of agent and purpose. Their focus is on the nature of prayer's human and divine agents as the authorizing ground of discourse. Prayer's purpose, consequently, is to realize divine-human relations through discourse. *Spiritual Modalities* neither supports nor challenges particular theologies in posing complementary questions about prayer as rhetorical performance. How is communication possible between human and divine beings? Where does this communication fit within a broader social order such that it matters profoundly if divine beings are not addressed? How to account for the range of practices, in various media, that can be identified as falling under a heading of "prayer"?

Burke's diverse contributions to rhetoric are only several strands among many that I bring to bear on prayer. These include the deliberate interplay between multiple rhetorical vocabularies, classical and modern, in their application to prayer, which, I would argue, is vital for advancing the larger project of *Spiritual Modalities*: to naturalize prayer within the purview of rhetoric. I do so by demonstrating in prayer a welcome receptivity to rhetorical inquiry. A governing principle in my project is to avoid reductive approaches to prayer, even at the risk of leaving the central term in prayer itself open, at some level, to productive misunderstanding.

The range of my representative texts and practices is consequently broad; I have selected these idiosyncratically, not primarily as objects of study in themselves but as illustrations of theoretical principles with which my account is concerned. I do not read texts presented here within particular traditions. Although these texts represent prayer beyond the traditions of monotheism, they could arguably range more widely still, across non-Western religions. Even so, the examples considered amply demonstrate prayer's phenomenal diversity.

Plan of the Book

Spiritual Modalities traces the cognitive, social, and material dimensions of prayer as a rhetorical art. Chapter 1 develops a rhetorical lexicon centered about twinned notions of need and opportunity to read prayer as a situational art. It pays particular attention to contemporary notions of exigence and to classical concepts of *kairos* and *krisis* as conceptual tools for locating discourse in a performative context. After surveying rhetorical approaches to situation by Lloyd Bitzer, Kenneth Burke, and Scott Consigny as fitting models for understanding prayer, it examines common typologies of prayer and explores notions of prayer as performative space. In particular, it argues for prayer as a space of "rehearsal for living," a space in which rhetors practice ethical subjectivity in relation to divine audiences. The chapter concludes with an extended reading of Reinhold Niebuhr's "Serenity Prayer" as an exemplary instance of prayer as discourse both situat*ed* and situat*ing*.

The first of three chapters centered in methods of dramatism drawn from Burke's *Grammar of Motives*, chapter 2 emphasizes the significance of prayer as a scene of address. It critiques Larry Dossey's *Healing Words* as a contemporary *anti*rhetoric of "prayer" (imagined as indirect, agentless action at a distance) to advance a detailed treatment of prayer as a complex auditory scene involving a range of *audiences* positioned as hearers and overhearers in relation to prayer's human speakers. Informed by Bakhtinian notions of addressivity in addition to Burkean notions of address, the chapter concludes by recognizing divine beings as perfect audiences for an experience of "being heard" in prayer. This experience serves meta-rhetorically as the principle underlying our human rhetorical potential.

Chapter 3 shifts focus from the scene-act relation in chapter 2 to the act-scene relation to examine prayer as the concrete performance of address. It argues that *invocation*, or the calling upon some unseen presence or power, is prayer's definitive speech act (just as address is its definitive scene) because, through invocation, human and divine beings are summoned into mutual presence. Beyond their capacity as summons, invocations strategically name and thereby channel divine agency. Reading Jonathan Culler on the "embarrassment" of apostrophe, the chapter explores distinctions between poetic and rhetorical acts of address, arguing for invocation as a rhetorical encounter with "the real." Finally, it turns to the ethics of invocation, by examining philosophers Emmanuel Levinas, Jacques Derrida, and Jean-Luc Marion on rhetorical approaches to invocation as a pragmatic and political act. It concludes by considering the capacity of invocation to call upon the *vocation* of its speakers to bring new situations into being.

Chapter 4 completes a conceptual arc established by the previous two chapters with the addition of *attitude* as a motivational term marking the *manner* of rhetorical performance. Through examination of attitude's psychosomatic character, the chapter argues for prayer as embodied performance. Specifically, prayer performs *reverence*, or the gracious acceptance of hierarchical relations. The chapter further illustrates the performative dynamics of reverence in the rhetoric of praise and closes with a close reading of a Kwakiutl ritual addressing the sockeye salmon, upon whose beneficence the Kwakiutl depend for their survival. This complex rhetorical situation extends notions of reverence beyond praise to the gods to consider rhetoric as an ethic of responsive and responsible discourse.

Chapter 5 situates the performative practices examined in preceding chapters in social and material settings of time and place. It identifies prayer as a rhetorical art of memory, the fourth of classical rhetoric's traditional canons. It argues that prayer is a socialized craft of both communication and commemoration. It closely reads a single prayer to Mary in Catholic tradition, the Memorare, for its illustrative range of memorial practices. Extending Paul Prior and Jody Shipka's notion of "chronotopic lamination" to prayer, the chapter concludes by marking prayer's memorial (and methodical) operations at multiple levels.

Finally, chapter 6 extends prayer beyond individual bodies through attention to classical rhetoric's canon of delivery. Exploring a dialectic between prayer as *said* and prayer as *sent*, the chapter considers the performative interface between prayer's speakers and audiences, especially in its migrating from embodied practices of oral performance to performances of virtual presence in textual and digital environments. It argues that prayer is a complex encounter with the real through the virtual, the spiritual through the material. This encounter long precedes digital modes of communication, but prayer finds its performative logic (as a rhetoric of delivery) intriguingly epitomized in just such communication. The chapter examines two representative websites that facilitate online prayer in order to articulate a model of prayer, and in particular intercessory prayer, as discourse in virtual motion connecting both human and divine agents in active models of community.

Spiritual Modalities' readings of select, but profound, dimensions of prayerful discourse together demonstrate that, by design, prayer assembles into performative wholes our human encounters with our potential as discursive beings. Never are we more ourselves as linguistically enabled, embodied beings than when we perform appeals to our counterparts in divine beings as manifestations of the real. The enabling assumption of my account is that prayer serves, above all, as a practical meta-rhetoric whose ultimate purpose is to sound out the limits and possibilities inherent in social cooperation imagined at its most thoroughgoing. This is prayer's implicit promise.

1

PRAYER AND ITS SITUATIONS:
MEDITATION ON *KAIROS* AND *KRISIS*

Situation emerged as a key term in rhetorical theory after Lloyd Bitzer employed it in his 1968 landmark essay "The Rhetorical Situation." Since then, notions of situation have been essential to rhetoric's self-understanding, distinguishing rhetoric from its near relations in philosophy and the human sciences. Whereas other disciplines articulate general principles underlying and informing human action and establish methodological norms to guide that articulation, rhetoric attends to the local, contextual, and contingent in human affairs. A bottom-up inquiry, rhetoric encounters discursive events not primarily as instances or confirmations of general principles but as singular occurrences rich in particularity and, if not inexhaustible in their range of significations, then indeterminate with respect to a definitive reading. As a matter of temperament, rhetoric sets itself against closure and certitude, for there is always more to be said and other ways to look at things.

Rhetoric insists on the provisional character of claims of ontology (what is) and epistemology (what can be known). Audaciously, rhetoric professes modesty, insisting on the locus of *possibility* over necessity in human endeavor. It has the upper hand, argues Nancy Struever, in the "unresolved tension between philosophy's necessitarian theses and rhetoric's anti-necessitarian practices" (6). Unlike philosophy, rhetoric grapples with modalities of possibility, actuality, and contingency: it "both defines and *poses* possibilities, both finds and creates, energizes possibilities" (7, emphasis in original). Connecting motive to method, Struever notes a "deep compatibility between the very specific analytic techniques rhetoric must develop to fulfill the demands of persuasion, the core political functions, and the very general commitment to the modality of possibility as the domain of rhetorical duty" (7).

With this disposition as backdrop, rhetoric's motive for insisting on the situated character of discourse becomes clear: to preserve human agency against all efforts to reduce its scope, including efforts to collapse the particular onto the general. In many ways a peculiar art, rhetoric relishes description, mindful that such symbolic efforts enliven experience. Yet even as it does so, it cautions itself not to read too much into any given situation.

Just as Struever compares rhetoric to philosophy, so we can compare prayer to theology. Prayer is a pragmatic art, one whose creative energy fuels possibilities for "the core political functions" governing relationships, in this case, between human and divine beings, socially significant otherworldly agents. A language of possibility by turns brazen in its power to shake the heavens and fretful over the risks, seductions, and limitations that attend this power, prayer mimetically represents the situations in which we, as human beings, find ourselves. Indeed, it may be claimed that prayer is par excellence a "rhetoric of situation," a means for discerning and articulating placement, both in the particularity of immediate circumstance and in the broader cosmos, where discovering one's place is the basis for ethical action.

In "Attention and Responsibility," philosopher Norman Wirzba approaches prayer from a phenomenological perspective, observing that "prayer is appropriately understood as the most intimate and honest means through which an understanding of our place in the universe can be achieved" (88–89). For Wirzba, the objective of prayer is profoundly simple: "to situate our life properly and justly among the lives of others" (89). This effort entails, first, an intellectual obligation to apprehend as accurately as possible the situations in which we find ourselves and, then, an ethical obligation to bring situations into conformity with justice. Wirzba's theologically inflected account frames prayer explicitly as "essential in the pursuit of truth" (89). Grounding prayer in paradigms of epistemic certainty and moral absolutes, Wirzba counters "postmodern" sensibilities of skepticism and relativism, perspectives on truth and knowledge that have marked rhetoric as a sophistic art concerned only with localized strategy. Yet his identification of prayer as a site where "epistemology and ethics meet" resonates with concerns central to rhetorical inquiry; his conception of prayer in heuristic terms strongly parallels Aristotle's foundational account of rhetoric as an art of discovery leading to practice.

In the case of prayer, the objective is not to discover the available means of persuasion in a given situation but, rather, the situation itself. Prayer is, first of all, an "art of situation": it is situated and situating discourse that speaks both from and to the conditions that give rise to its occasions as utterance. Benefiting from as well as complicating an established range of perspectives on rhetoric as situational, in particular those of Lloyd Bitzer and Kenneth Burke in different strands of a U.S. rhetorical tradition, such a reading challenges the dominance of a situational perspective in rhetoric by recognizing the significance of "space" as well as "time" in the rhetorical construction of situations. To that end, this chapter brings a range of concepts into play, including ways of marking time rhetorically in the classical notions of kairos and krisis and the contemporary notions of exigence and response.

Situating Prayer in Time and Space

A familiar call to assembly in many religious contexts, "Let us pray" may be voiced in song, as in the musical intonations of the muezzin calling faithful Moslems to prayer, or in the peal of bells announcing the hours of devotion. Through such acts of invitation is a religious community oriented to devotional purposes at prescribed intervals or on impromptu occasions. A summons to prayer, even at its most informal, marks a ritual moment. It is also a liminal moment that separates prayer's time from ordinary time. The call to prayer signals possibilities that lie ahead and supposes that something will come of embracing the moment. Prayer, in other words, is experienced as a moment of both opportunity (kairos) and decision (krisis).

Shot through as it is with critical and kairotic sensibilities, prayer is often less what is experienced at a particular moment than the moment itself, bracketed off from the ordinary. Devotion is paid in the currency of time. Moments in the pregnant call to prayer are properly inaugural: they represent critical turning points or renewed opportunities. Prayer is largely cyclic or iterative in conforming to social rhythms, such as the five daily calls to worship in Islam, saying grace before meals, and commemorating milestones in personal or civic life. Not least among prayer's purposes is to mark occasions as significant.

Because human attention, the "engine" of prayer, inevitably wanes, moments for human and divine commerce opened by prayer continually resolve into ordinary time. Effort is required to maintain and to reestablish these moments, much as additional torque is needed to keep a top spinning. A call to prayer from without thus has its counterpart in efforts to pay attention as a form of self-summons. Whatever form this summons may take, it signals a moment when prayer is *called for*, telling would-be rhetors that here is a situation for which prayer is the appropriate response. This call is experienced as an *exigence*—an "imperfection marked by urgency"—demanding response (Bitzer 6).

The concept of exigence is particularly associated with Lloyd Bitzer and the debate sparked by "The Rhetorical Situation." Bitzer's crucial insight is that situations are rhetorical when an exigence "is capable of positive modification and when positive modification requires discourse or can be assisted by discourse" (6). For Bitzer, situations have three constituent elements—exigence, audience, and constraints—which are "prior to the creation and presentation of discourse" (6). This last point has received the greatest criticism from those who would challenge Bitzer's objectivist account of situation and response.

A neat subjectivist counter to Bitzer is Richard Vatz's essay "The Myth of the Rhetorical Situation," which holds that discourse creates situations rather than responds to them: "No situation can have a nature independent of the perception of its interpreter or independent of the rhetoric with which he chooses to characterize it" (154). In a similar vein, Alan Brinton observes that, though Bitzer imagines a fitting, and hence normative, response to situations, responses are rhetorical only to the extent they modify the exigence that demands them.

In "Rhetoric and Its Situations" (whose title prefigures this chapter), Scott Consigny challenges the Bitzer-Vatz opposition of objectivity and subjectivity, deterministic and "free" approaches to situation, calling instead for a "topical" approach to rhetoric as situated discourse. In Consigny's view, rhetorical acts negotiate between topics as "places" and "tools of inquiry": "If either of the two meanings of topic is ignored, and the topic becomes either a mere situation or a mere instrument, the coherence of the rhetorical act breaks down, for there is no way to account for the engagement of the rhetor in the situation" (182). Consigny's account of situation is especially relevant to prayer in recognizing situations as both a frame for and a construction of discourse. Conceived as a response to a call, prayer is neither "mere situation" nor "mere instrument," but a creative fusion in which place (topos) is nonetheless central.

In defining a rhetorical situation as "a complex of persons, events, objects, and relations presenting an actual or potential exigence which can be completely or partially removed if discourse, introduced into the situation, can so constrain human decision or action as to bring about the significant modification of the exigence," Bitzer most likely did not have prayer in mind (6). Indeed, his definition fails to include divine agents among those whose decisions and actions may be constrained through discourse. More important, his understanding of rhetorical exigence as something "completely or partially removed" through discourse is not easily squared with communicative events that construct, maintain, and deepen relationships between interlocutors. Bitzer's exigence is an uncomfortable fit for imagining prayer as a rhetorical response. To be sure, if divine audiences are to be included in his definition, then notions of exigence have some utility in contexts where specific things are prayed for. On the other hand, emphasis on exigence as a crucial element of a rhetorical situation must be balanced by a complementary recognition of kairotic opportunity and ethical obligation.

A far more resonant notion for the situations in which prayer is a proper response, kairos signals the dynamic possibility in moments of opportunity for action. As Phillip Sipiora observes, the classical concept of kairos evolved into a rich profusion of concepts involving timeliness, fit, and proportion, besides opportunity (1). In *Bodily Arts*, an account of the relationship between rhetoric and athletics in ancient Greece, Debra Hawhee identifies kairos as "embodied time," personified in the divinity of Kairos, youngest son of Zeus (11). Dale Sullivan, in "Kairos and the Rhetoric of Belief," recognizes that a "sense of ripening" attaches to notions of kairos in human and divine interaction—an understanding of kairos as God's time (322). A critical moment calls for decisive judgment. A kairotic moment recognizes an opportunity to act.[1]

Notions of opportunity (kairos) and judgment (krisis) present an intriguing parallel to the dynamic relationship of attention and responsibility that Norman Wirzba considers the systole and diastole of prayer's beating heart. Yet another parallel is to be found in the sermons of Jesuit theologian Karl Rahner as collected in *The Need and the Blessing of Prayer*. Addressing a Munich devastated by war, Rahner identifies the situation of modernity: for many, prayer, a language of possibility, has become impossible. Tracing the contours of despair, which he likens to living one's days in a bombed-out cellar, Rahner speaks of survivors going through the motions: "People with this chronic despair remain in control of themselves, they remain quite normal and everyday. They conduct themselves as all reasonable people conduct themselves. . . . But all that is only a facade. All this is only supposed to cover up the innermost, the deepest point of the heart, the wound of the heart from which one slowly bleeds to death, about which one doesn't talk because of propriety (a proper and educated human being is not supposed to despair)" (5). As befits a Christian text, Rahner imagines a kairotic opening in a radical receptivity to God's love. Experience of need opens one to prayer, and prayer becomes an experience of *blessing*. Discovering prayer is equivalent to discovering our real situation in the world. Rahner's placement of critical need and blessed opportunity into dynamic relation, where prayer is both a critical response to an exigence and a creative act that leads to discovery of our real situation, echoes Consigny's insight of rhetoric as a site of negotiation between situations and tools.

What, then, is the rhetorical situation of prayer? Following Rahner, we might characterize it in terms of an existential crisis or a profound experience of opening in response to opportunity. Yet, if rhetoric is to be equated with the local and particular, how could prayer have a single situation? Do situations welcome multiple responses, or does every situation correspond to some particular response? Although no definitive answer is forthcoming, I suggest it is useful to imagine situations on a spectrum ranging from the singular to the infinitely many. Indeed, where we locate prayer on this situational spectrum reveals much about how we understand rhetorical action.

The number of prayer's situations is relevant to Kenneth Burke's understanding of rhetorical situation: In "The Philosophy of Literary Form," he observes that "critical and imaginative works are answers to questions posed by the situation in which they arose. They are not merely answers, they are *strategic* answers, *stylized* answers" (*PLF* 1, emphasis in original). They involve the "adopting of various strategies for the encompassing of situations. . . . These strategies size up the situations, name their structure and outstanding ingredients, and name them in a way that contains an attitude towards them" (1). A stylized answer in the language of prayer implies one situation; a different strategy, a different situation. Burke characterizes the nature and scope of situations: "Situations do overlap, if only because men now have the same neural and muscular structure as men who have left their records from past ages. We and they are in much the same biological situation. . . . And the nature of the human mind itself, with the function of abstraction rooted in the nature of language, also provides us with 'levels of generalization' (to employ Korzybski's term) by which situations greatly different in their particularities may be felt to belong in the same class (to have a common substance or essence)" (2). In Burke's view, we cannot help but see some situations in categorical relation to others. In prayer, as with other discourse, we share in broader situations, rooted in our biological and social constitutions and reflected in our stylized answers.

The belief that situations recur has been central to rhetoric since Aristotle, who proposes three generalized speech situations: epideictic, forensic, and deliberative discourse (1.3). Insofar as prayer is a *civic* art, it may be assigned to one (or more) of these domains. Depending on the context, prayer performs ceremonial functions associated with the *epideictic* in expressing shared values and forging collective identity; the critical functions of the *forensic* in discerning causes and conditions; and the persuasive functions of the *deliberative* in influencing future actions of people and of deities.

In "Performativity and Persuasion in the Hebrew Book of Psalms," Davida Charney proposes that the psalms "can be seen as arguments posed to God by Israelites, sometimes as individuals and sometimes as a community, over the continuation of their covenantal relationship" (248). Reading specific psalms, Charney demonstrates "how psalmists develop well-supported claims intended to move God to action" (251). By fusing poetic and rhetorical motives, the psalms function as a repertoire of rhetorical strategies for use in concrete contexts of temple worship. Within Jewish and Christian tradition, they remain an indispensable resource for understanding characteristic situations in which prayer's performers organize prayer into genres of performance for devotional purposes. In identifying psalms as "oral public poetry," with suggestive parallels to Greek civic oratory, Charney recognizes classification schemes, whether Aristotelian or other, as rhetorical constructions (248).

Prayer has been subjected to typologies ranging from form-critical approaches to biblical texts to less scholarly and explicitly motivational typologies, all reflecting tensions between situational and strategic approaches to discourse.[2] These include the common typology of prayer according to its four primary aims—petition, praise, thanksgiving, and confession—which may be considered distinct, stand-alone genres or performative moves of what can be said or done in prayer. In the terms of speech-act theory, these moves exert force upon one or both of prayer's interlocutors. Additional moves include lament and accusation, as well as blessing and cursing, which channel divine power. Within this typology, further distinctions, such as petition for oneself versus petition for others, recognize the multiplicity of situations for which these primary moves serve as response.

Here it is important to note that these formal and functional typologies are not objective characterizations but *models* of practice. As normative models, they theorize prayer in situational terms, placing those who pray in a particular mode *in the same situation* as others. The critical task is to understand prayer as a set of strategies for sizing up situations. For heuristic purposes, I propose an axial model, plotting situation against strategy to capture a vital sense of dimensionality in prayer. In this model, speech settings on the horizontal axis establish what *must* be said in prayer, while speech acts on the vertical axis shape what *may* be said, opportunistically, in prayer. The model's axial coordinates define a set of things to do with prayer. Echoing J. L. Austin, I suggest that a basic set of speech acts, largely preserved across horizontal contexts, defines relationships between prayer's human and divine agents.

Whereas prayer's forms vary greatly, prayer's *acts* are fairly circumscribed: only certain kinds of statements, principally about relations between speaker and spoken-to, effectively count as prayer. Through a range of performatives, prayer's speakers establish and maintain relationships with divine beings as well as exert leverage on the basis of these relationships. Prayer's characteristic speech moves are highly adaptive to specific performative contexts and to available media. They shape and transform the situations in which they are embedded.

In plotting coordinates of setting and act, I express in more schematic terms the insight that prayer is both situated and situational. Here I echo Consigny's claim that topics of discourse are at once situation and tool and Burke's claim that situation and strategy are not, finally, isolable but must always be "plotted" together. I further counter Bitzer's belief that situations are always prior to discourse. Another way to interpret this axial model is to see that, on its horizontal axis, human conditions and social interactions define social settings and, on its vertical axis, discourse, oriented upward, defines relations between the human and the divine. Prayerful actions, by their very nature, are multidimensional. The model emphasizes that prayer performs in both horizontal and vertical dimensions. Consequently, it cannot be understood apart from its character as a social act in horizontal (human) terms and cannot be "flattened" to the horizontal simply by disregarding its vertical dimension. Although prayer's horizontal dimension may be more pronounced in certain lights and less in others, the key to any analysis is to recognize that prayer's situations are multidimensional.

Rhetorical Situation, Performative Space

A distinctive feature of prayer is the degree to which it performs its situation. Take this familiar yet strange bedtime prayer from childhood:

> Now I lay me down to sleep.
> I pray the Lord my soul to keep.
> If I die before I wake,
> I pray the Lord my soul to take.

Arguably, the prayer's strangest element is not its invocation of death but, rather, its stylized performance of context: it spells out its setting, action, and objective in a seemingly magical effort to ward off the unthinkable. Much prayer resembles this not-so-simple text in its use of metadiscourse to position speaker and spoken-to.

Such conversion of context into text is most evident in prayers of petition, which not only voice specific needs but also supply warrants to justify why a petition should be granted. These warrants may invoke a divine being's power to grant certain requests ("You have the power to do something"); they may remind the being of prior beneficence ("You have done this before"); they may offer promises ("If you do this for me, I will do this for you"); or they may appeal to the being's sense of reputation ("Do this and your name will be glorified"). Prayers of praise and thanksgiving likewise name their situation in supplying reasons to render thanks or praise. Not everything is spelled out in prayer, however. In the bedtime prayer cited above, horizontal (human-human) contexts of family bonding and moral instruction are left unspoken. In this and most other cases, prayer's horizontal contexts are described only as they inform its vertical (human-divine) purposes.

A classic African American spiritual hymn, "Standing in the Need of Prayer," testifies to prayer's necessity and blessing:[3]

> It's me, It's me,
> It's me, O Lord
> Standin' in the need of prayer
> 'Taint my mother or my father,
> But it's me, O Lord
> Standin' in the need of prayer. (Moore 113)

The hymn dramatizes a scene of utterance with a motif that announces a praying self—"It's me, O Lord." It locates performers psychologically and physically, as singers standing and announcing that they stand in the need of prayer. Though sung in a congregational setting, the hymn foregrounds *individual* utterance. Each singer confesses a unique estrangement from the Lord to be overcome through acknowledgment *to* the Lord. The element of witness complicates the articulated scene of one-on-one communication between human speaker and divine audience. The prayer is at once a communal act performed at a particular place and time and a dramatic rendering of a universal condition of dependency.

Additional verses of "Standing" distinguish the hymn's performer from sib-lings and clergy to further emphasize the performer's individual praying self. As this hymn demonstrates, congregational prayer need not take the "we" form. More generally, a hymn accommodates departures from an immediate con-text of utterance to imagine dramatic spaces in which performance is stylized to articulate both collective and individual experience. Although this hymn's performers need not experience "standing in the need of prayer" to sing this hymn, they might yet perform themselves *into* this insight. "Standing" articu-lates a devotional commonplace—one always stands in the need of prayer—to be given lip service or embraced as an experiential truth. Such commonplaces are an inventional resource for discerning and performing situations.

These performative moves, at their most formal, map discourse to situation through the resources of genre. As a middle ground between one and uncount-ably many situations, genres aggregate discrete situations by virtue of overlap-ping contexts and recurring features. Depending on how fine the distinctions are, genres of prayer conceivably number in the hundreds. They range from occasion-based genres (grace before meals) and acts of address directed to par-ticular divinities (angels, saints, ancestors) to genres associated with specific rites such as the Collect in the Catholic or Anglican liturgy or the Jewish *berakhah*, as a formulary for blessings. Without a robust sense of genre, prayer would be literally unimaginable. With genre, prayer becomes a finely tuned instrument for activating a network of social relationships through discourse. A typology of prayer such as petition, praise, and thanksgiving roughly sorts prayer into performative genres insofar as form may be wedded to function.

Carolyn Miller shifts attention from form to function in her highly influ-ential "Genre as Social Action." Building off Bitzerian and Burkean notions of situation, Miller offers a social constructionist reading of genre as "typified rhetorical actions based in recurrent situations" (159). Genre thus refers to what people do with forms, not to the forms themselves. Every genre performs in that it operates through form in a social context. Genres emerge, transform, and even disappear as contexts are modified by social or technological change. Miller's notion that genres create situations as much as situations create genres parallels the notion I am advancing here that the relationship between the rhe-torical acts of prayer and the situations to which they respond is constructively indeterminate. Prayer is as much devoted to interpreting situations, to discern-ing "what ends we may have" in Miller's terms (165), as it is to responding to particular exigencies.

Prayer as Rehearsal for Living

Having identified prayer as a response to situational givens, circumstantial in its immediate, horizontal (human-human) settings and existential in its vertical (human-divine) relations, let us turn to matters of prayer and location in a different sense. The situational givens of critical need and kairotic opportunity frame prayer, in Wirzba's terms, as a dialectic of "attention" and "responsibility." To attend carefully and to respond fittingly to one's real situation in an ordered cosmos is prayer's critical and ethical task. To understand prayer in these terms, we need to shift our attention from site to *space*: prayer expresses a sense of place in an ordered cosmos by negotiating between different orders of existence. Occurring within a frame, prayer is itself a frame—a space we may enter and leave and within which we may abide.

In developing this spatial notion, we might first consider a related *temporal* notion in Christian tradition of prayer as ceaseless. This perspective is given substance in Saint Paul's exhortation: "Rejoice always, pray without ceasing, give thanks in all circumstances" (1 Thess. 5:16–18), behind which is the insight that prayer is more *state* than statement, a matter of ongoing condition rather than episodic activity. "'Unceasing prayer' has two meanings in Scripture," writes theologian John Wright (qtd. in Giardini 336): "frequently repeated acts of prayer, returning again and again to praise, thank, and petition God" and "an ongoing quality of life, even outside times of formal prayer. The express activity of formal prayer overflows to communicate a quality of prayer in the whole of one's life." Unceasing prayer recognizes that expression is ephemeral; it longs to open the bounded space of a communicative act and to transform it into something permanent.

One need not take Saint Paul literally here. Paul would cultivate desire for God through habit so that prayer is genuine and ongoing and not a sometime thing or last resort when all else fails. Prayer is thus imagined as a basic orientation toward the source of one's being. Repeated acts may be indispensable for cultivating this orientation, but prayer is not reducible to act. The charge to "pray without ceasing," to be fully present in any communicative act, requires considerable effort.

Two views of prayer as discourse are brought together here. In one, prayer is a timeless space irrespective of immediate occasion. Within this view, prayer is always opportune, the conditions that warrant it always relevant. Though prayer adjusts to exigent circumstances and kairotic moments in appropriate genres, its governing imperative (to be in discursive relationship with the divine) does not change. Thus understood, only the constraints of human frailty prevent full embrace of prayer's boundless kairos. In a second, more conventional view, however, prayer is bounded as discourse performed in time. Like any discourse, it responds to circumstances as a means to an end, not an end in itself. In this alternative view, prayer is serious play—an earnest drama in which human beings negotiate with their divine counterparts as best they can.

A tension between bounded and unbounded time is central to prayer as a rhetorical act. Translated into a secular idiom and from temporal to spatial frames, the call to pray without ceasing is a call to inhabit an alternative frame—an *extra*ordinary space (with otherworldly beings and distinct rules of engagement). This space serves as a corrective to discourse within ordinary space.

But even though prayer is shot through with motives it shares with other discourse, it occupies a peculiar place in relation to other rhetorical acts. For prayer is not only a distinct space in which human and divine beings establish contact; it is also a meta-rhetorical space of *rehearsal*. That is to say, prayer functions as a space of retreat and recalibration in which aspects of communication and performance (such as ethos and agency) are "worked out" through *practice*. Prayer is a space in which rhetoric is tested and trued. By a fortunate accident of spelling, "rehearse" suggests a false etymology: rehearing—the better to master a part. This association works to advantage since rehearsal points to conditioning dimensions of training for increased capability. Rehearsal is typically shielded from view; behind the scenes, it leads to progressive improvement for future performance.

In this respect, I suggest, prayer serves as a space of "rehearsal for living," an expression inspired by Kenneth Burke's essay "Literature as Equipment for Living," where he observes that proverbs "size up" "typical, recurrent situations," and literature serves similar didactic ends (*PLF* 293). Arguing that "the most complex and sophisticated works of art" might "legitimately be considered somewhat as 'proverbs writ large'" (297), Burke asserts a necessarily braided relationship between rhetoric and poetics: the ethical and the aesthetic are not credibly separated on the basis of inherent properties of texts.

Burke's sociological criticism suggests close connections between poem, proverb, and prayer. Like proverbs, prayers structure daily living through a pious embodiment of attitude. Also like proverbs, prayers name their situations as a spur to future action. Prayer steels its performers to challenges and steers them to appropriate practices. In a typology striking for its religious cast, Burke notes literature's social functions "for selecting enemies and allies, for socializing

losses, for warding off the evil eye, for purification, propitiation and desanctifi-
cation, consolation and vengeance, admonition and exhortation, implicit com-
mands or instructions of one sort or another" (*PLF* 304). This enumeration of
literature's social moves reveals its essentially prayerful dimension and is consistent with Burke's "subdivisions for the analysis of an act in poetry"—"chart,"
"prayer," and "dream"—introduced in *The Philosophy of Literary Form*, where he
comes closest to identifying prayer *as* rhetoric:

> Chart: "the realistic sizing-up of situations that is sometimes explicit,
>   sometimes implicit, in poetic strategies";
> Prayer: "the communicative function of the poem";
> Dream: "the unconscious or subconscious factors in a poem" (*PLF* 5–6).

The strategic or social functions of literature are a fusion of these "interwoven"
elements, with a pronounced tilt toward "chart" in that proverbs are particularly
invested in sizing up situations (5). In this scheme, prayer itself manifests each
of these dimensions but especially the "communicative" functions assigned the
label of "prayer."[4]

One can regard prayer as having this precise purpose: to shape character by
orienting performers to present and future action by manifesting a communicative self. Indeed, Burke echoes a long line of religious observers in announcing
that "the man who does not 'pray' cannot build his character" (*ATH* 322). He
refers to "secular prayer," consistent with a habit of applying terms oxymoroni-
cally across domains—his method of "perspective by incongruity" (308). "Secular prayer is usually called 'word magic' by those who think they can propose
contrivances for its elimination"; such contrivances are themselves "examples of
prayer, albeit in disguise" (321). The core functions of prayer—regulation, reas-
surance, resolution—are not avoided in secular prayer, merely translated into
another idiom. Prayer, for Burke, is socialized apprehension of some emergent
reality, a discursive act that calls something into existence. It may be likened
to the activity of children whose play involves "*naming the essence* of their play
objects, assigning names that violate realistic identity," by which "discounting"
one "transcends" brute "material reality" (322, emphasis in original).

These strategic acts may profitably be understood as rehearsal for living. They
are practices to be integrated into an ethically engaged subjectivity. In this context, it hardly trivializes prayer to regard it as a mode of sophisticated play in
which divine beings now assume the roles formerly held by objects in a child's

imagination. Quite the contrary, to play in this way is not to pretend; it is to imagine through topoi of possibility. Burke's primary insight here is that such practiced, practical activity is properly dramatic. Prayer takes place in a space of performance essential to the formation of individual and social character.

The sacred space of prayer, opened and closed by ritual expressions such as "Let us pray" and "Amen," is often located in churches, mosques, and temples, where material space reifies conceptual space. Here I argue that prayer involves periodic habitation of an alternative space that requires substantial mediation to exploit its communicative potential. This mediation varies both across and within performative traditions regarding how the space of prayer is configured and thus accessed. It may be imagined as having high or low barriers to entry or levels between which prayer is a journey upward or inward, from ordinary to extraordinary space. Many didactic and devotional works have charted prayer's spiritual terrain through spatial metaphors. Among the most memorable are those of Teresa of Avila, whose classic accounts of prayer in *The Way of Perfection* and *The Interior Castle* illuminate paths and structures to dramatize spiritual development toward union with God.

It is also possible to reverse the priority of relationships between performative spaces by regarding ordinary space as rehearsal and prayer as final performance. In this entelechial reading of prayer, we practice relating with other human beings in order to relate, ultimately, to God. Irrespective of the priority assigned to these complementary spaces, prayer obtains its rhetorical character precisely from their interaction. The value of prayer as a performative space follows from its character as a space accessible to ordinary space, yet sufficiently removed that its entering or leaving marks a ritual passage. This value depends, too, on perceived ethical relations between the spaces, on how acts performed in the marked space of prayer relate to those in its unmarked counterpart. Characterizing prayer as a space of rehearsal (with dual connotations of practice and hearing) emphasizes prayer as a manifestation of the ethical in Burke's character-building sense.

Rhetorical Situation of the "Serenity Prayer"

Given the enormous influence of Emile Durkheim's structuralist account of religion in *The Elementary Forms of the Religious Life*, it is tempting to identify as "profane" that space where prayer, as sacred space, is not. Yet the conceptual spaces marked by prayer are not so dichotomous as this sacred-profane binary would suggest. Topologically, these spaces are *interlaced*, their boundaries blending into each other even as they remain conceptually distinct. By design, the performative spaces in which human and divine communication occurs have an impact on relationships in a strictly human space. Indeed, it is the possibility for transcendence and for transformation represented by the space of prayer that bestows value.

For an illustration of prayer as a dynamic space of rehearsal, let us turn to the familiar "Serenity Prayer," attributed to U.S. theologian Reinhold Niebuhr but, more often, associated with Alcoholics Anonymous (AA). According to Elizabeth Sifton, Niebuhr's daughter, the "Serenity Prayer" was composed in the summer of 1943 in Heath, Massachusetts, in the context of a world at war.[5] In 1944, Niebuhr permitted its inclusion in materials for army field chaplains prepared by the Federal Council of Churches, and it was in Europe that the prayer first caught on (Sifton 292). Niebuhr later allowed AA liberal use of a simplified, and now more familiar, version of the prayer: "God, grant me the serenity to accept the things I cannot change, the courage to change the things I can, and the wisdom to know the difference" (Linn 5). Frequently appended to this or an alternate version—"God, give us grace to accept with serenity the things that cannot be changed, courage to change the things which should be changed, and the wisdom to discern the one from the other" (Sifton 14)—are the following lines of unknown authorship:

> Living one day at a time;
> enjoying one moment at a time;
> accepting hardship as the pathway to peace.
> Taking, as He did, this sinful world as it is, not as I would have it,
> Trusting that He will make all things right if I surrender to His will.
> That I may be reasonably happy in this life
> and supremely happy with Him forever in the next. Amen. (Linn 5)

Arguably the most popular of modern prayers, the "Serenity Prayer" exemplifies notions of rehearsal as well as reliance on proverbial and character-building capacities of discourse. Beginning in address to "God," the prayer dramatizes an ethical stance as much as it manifests a speech act of entreaty. What virtues it asks for in "grace," "courage," and "wisdom" are not things easily obtained for the asking. Indeed, the prayer's reflective character as a petition for virtues, rather than for specific things or outcomes, makes it suitable across a full range of individual contexts.[6] In principle, anyone can discover him- or herself in the situation represented by the prayer. Indeed, the prayer enables one to recognize one's situation in and through the text. Above all, the prayer opens a space of discernment as prelude to action. It meets its performers where they *are*, providing opportunities for spiritual assessment and development.

Appealing to a higher power as a source of virtue, the "Serenity Prayer" transcends mere affirmation. It opens a space for performers both to mend and to prepare with respect to challenges outside that space. Although few prayers construct so generic a space of retreat, many prayers share with the "Serenity Prayer" a capacity to subsume concrete situations outside and abstract situations inside themselves—the better to imagine a potential self over against a present one. The "Serenity Prayer" is pointedly kairotic in its explicit call for wisdom by which to gauge situations. Because the prayer lacks many of the contextual features that articulate relations between human and divine, its meta-rhetorical character as a rehearsal space for ethical action is especially pronounced. As with other prayers, a double sense of rehearsal attends this prayer. It is a text to be performed and a space to be entered repeatedly.

The prayer implicit in *all* prayer as a strategy for encompassing the real is that our prayers be accurate. In the "Serenity Prayer," this governing subtext is explicitly thematized in "the wisdom to discern" the difference between things that should and can be changed and things that cannot. Implicit in this prayer is the understanding that prayer *in general* situates human and natural events in a larger drama by acquiring perspectives ever more accurate. If we are to act, we must know what our real situation is. The "Serenity Prayer" is, above all, a prayer for situational discernment. As Kenneth Burke observes, our "prayers can be extremely accurate, just as they can be extremely inaccurate," adding that "people usually reserve the words 'magic' or 'prayer' for the inaccurate ones alone" (*ATH* 324). Accuracy comes down, finally, to naming ingredients of our environment as an act of rehearsal, so that naming shapes action. In the terms of the "Serenity Prayer," this naming involves both strategies of acceptance for "the things that cannot be changed" and complementary strategies of courage in changing "the things that should [and can] be changed."

Burke's "Dialectician's Hymn" echoes and is instructively paired with Niebuhr's "Serenity Prayer":

> May we give true voice
> To the statements of Thy creatures.

May our spoken words speak for them,
With accuracy. . . .

May we compete with one another,
To speak for thy Creation with more justice—
Cooperating in this competition
Until our naming
Gives voice correctly.
And how things are
And how we say things are
Are one. (*PLF* 448–49)

As Burke cautions his readers in *The Philosophy of Literary Form*, any "distinction between belief, make-believe, and mock-belief [in this hymn] is left fluctuant" (448). Its key word, of course, is "may"—prayer's quintessential stylistic move and the essence of rhetoric's modal character in bridging actual and possible situations. The opening "May" and its complement, the closing "Amen," call situations into *being*, even at the risk of inaccurate perspectives. What "may" come must be selectively imagined. The implicit prayer in any prayer, again, is that it be *sufficiently* accurate to warrant "Amen" in word and deed.

This matter of accuracy in prayer comes full circle with kairos, for kairos also means proper measure. One must take stock of situations, see them accurately, if one is to respond effectively. Although prayer's rhetorical burden is accuracy, it is also discourse *upward*. It must err; prayer prays that it may be in the right direction. Writing on Burke's "Four Master Tropes," David Tell observes a crucial distinction between two often confused tropes: the reduction of metonymy and the representation of synecdoche. A "corrective for metonymic excess," Tell argues, synecdoche rescues discourse from a lack of measure (43): "It is synecdochic conversion upwards that 'induces' an audience to overcome the limitations of language" (44). Without this possibility of conversion upward by an adjustment of interpretive frames, situations can never be *more* than they are. Indeed, they must become *less* than they are since it is impossible for situations to remain in stasis. Burke's alignment of "how things are and how we say things are" is in this respect a prayerful, if also playful, call for an accurate and ethical rhetoric (*PLF* 449).

Burke's "Dialectician's Hymn" underscores that how situations are characterized determines *what* situations may be brought into being. For example, a prayer for peace may itself begin the work of peace. As Burke continues his hymn:

If the soil is carried off by the flood
May we help the soil to say so,
If our ways of living
Violate the needs of nerve and muscle,
May we find speech for nerve and muscle,
To frame objections
Whereat we, listening,
Can remake our habits (*PLF* 449).

These identifications of trauma to land and body, for we human beings must speak them, demonstrate that we may go only so far in exercising the optative. Reality being recalcitrant, our capacity to remake the universe as we might wish it is limited (*PC* 255). We must learn, therefore, to exercise that capacity responsibly to exploit the space between linguistic and material reality. This space is the realm of rhetoric.

Efforts to locate prayer in mere wish, then, are hopelessly reductive. Quite literally so, for such perspectives lack hope as the essential ingredient for ethical action, reducing the realm of possibility by a failure to see the whole picture. Burke's poetic dimensions of dream, prayer, and chart in any discursive act point to a fundamental distinction between the rhetoric of prayer and the symbolic of dream: prayer, the communicative dimension of the poetic act, is always an exercise in social cooperation with human others and with the powers above.

As articulated in the "Serenity Prayer," prayer's situation is ultimately one of hope. As an instrument of hope, prayer is both a capacity and a tool for discerning which situations are, finally, rhetorical and thus kairotic moments for ethical engagement. This sense of kairos as always open to possibility is perhaps what Saint Paul had in mind in exhorting Christians to pray ceaselessly. Relationships, if not acted on, quickly calcify. Paul recognized that one never knows when kairos, or opportunity, will again pass by. Even language soon calcifies when it no longer accurately describes the dynamic situations in which speakers find themselves, when prayer no longer enters into an alternative space of rehearsal.

Between the One and the Many

How, then, to number prayer's situations: in singular terms or as uncountably many? Although I advance no definitive answer to this question, I propose instead that the most profound problem we face with respect to prayer is not that it goes unanswered but that it goes unsaid. This is not a call for a return to any particular piety, however. It is, rather, an observation that in efforts to map prayers to situations, it may be that there are far more situations for prayer than there are prayers for situations. In suggesting this possibility, I take seriously Bitzer's notion that rhetorical situations by their nature demand rhetorical responses. Realistically speaking, we live with an abundance of *missed* opportunities to imagine and to call into being new orders and relations. A call to prayer may go unanswered or may be responded to unimaginatively. More often than not, we protect ourselves from invitations to pray, lest doing so require of us "the courage to change the things that should be changed." We are invested in metonymic *under*estimation of the situations calling for our prayers.

At the same time, we may overestimate prayer's situations through failure to generalize properly. At a sufficient distance, we might conclude that this prayer and that prayer are the *same* prayer, despite different situational ingredients. This is not to say diverse roads lead to a single divinity but to think kairotically about prayer as genre. Through metonymic mergers, the number of prayers may be continually reduced, until the set of prayers narrows considerably, if not quite to singularity. This set might roughly correspond to the range of positions human beings adopt in the face of common experiences of dependence. It might resemble a taxonomy of speech acts encoding experiences of affiliation and estrangement, want and satiety.

Taking these mergers yet further, we can say, with Burke, that prayer manifests "frames of acceptance and rejection" (*ATH* 5). They answer yes or no to a fundamental question at any given moment: Do we exist in a spirit of cooperation with the cosmos? Perhaps this takes things too far. There are degrees of abstraction few would wish and fewer still would hope to achieve. The realm of mystics, in which all linguistic divisions dissolve in an essential unity, is not for the faint of heart. Still, it is the business of prayer to seek higher ground where division may be transcended, where distinct situations are melded into more comprehensive unities. The closing lines of Burke's "Dialectician's Hymn" sum up this dialectic:

> And may we have neither the mania of the One
> Nor the delirium of the Many—
> But both the Union and the Diversity—
> The Title and the manifold details that arise

As that Title is restated
In the narrative of History. . . .
For us
Thy name a Great Synecdoche
Thy works a Grand Tautology. (*PLF* 450)

Although rhetoric is an art of the particular, prayer leans instinctively toward greater unity. Nonetheless, the recalcitrant character of our biology and, beyond that, the linguistic principle of division push back against this holistic tendency, so that prayer becomes a dialectic of opposing impulses—the yin of division and the yang of union. To a great extent, we decide to find ourselves in the same situations as others or in a unique situation. In its character as a meta-rhetoric, prayer is about the task of discovering the situations that we decide we are in.

Rhetoric insists both that necessity may be transcended in the discursive embrace of possibility and that the open-ended space of kairos trumps the closed circle of krisis. I have argued here that "prayer" is the appropriately opportunistic name for the rhetorical strategies by which we discern and act upon possibilities for transcendence and transformation, possibilities implicit within situations. Prayer's key strategy and animating impulse is that situations may be conceived in *dialogic* terms through appeal to divine beings as manifestations of the real. At the same time, it is both necessary and possible to make peace with—to "accept with serenity"—limitations to agency we discover in our encounters with the real. Prayer is nothing if not realistic in what it hopes may be achieved *by* hope, by entering alternative spaces that encompass situational possibilities.

In this chapter, I have argued that prayer is a multidimensional performative space of rehearsal centered in attention and responsibility as the criteria for ethical action. In the chapters to follow, I turn from prayer as situation to prayer as *strategy* and look to motivational elements of Burkean dramatism as points of departure for how prayer responds to the situations it encounters and calls into being.

2

"HEAR US, O LORD":
AUDIENCE AND ADDRESS
IN COMMUNICATING WITH THE DIVINE

> It is a principle of drama that the nature of acts and agents should
> be consistent with the nature of the scene.
>
> —Kenneth Burke, *A Grammar of Motives*

> The prayer preceding all prayers is, "May it be the real I who speaks.
> May it be the real Thou that I speak to."
>
> —C. S. Lewis, *Letters to Malcolm: Chiefly on Prayer*

One of the most dramatic moments in the *Iliad* occurs at the very beginning. The Greeks have waged a protracted siege against Troy. Chryses, a priest of Apollo, approaches Agamemnon to demand the release of his daughter, Chryseis, captured as a prize of war. When Agamemnon refuses, heaping scorn on him, a wrathful Chryses prays to his divine patron:

> Hear me, Apollo, God of the Silver bow
> Who strides the walls of Chryse and Cilla sacrosanct—
> lord in power of Tenedos—Smintheus, god of the plague!
>
> If I ever roofed a shrine to please your heart,
> ever burned the long rich bones of bulls and goats
> on your holy altar, now, now bring my prayer to pass.
> Pay the Danaans back—your arrows for my tears! (1.35–42)

His prayer is successful. On hearing this entreaty, delivered more as demand than request, Apollo exacts vengeance on the Greeks with a plague that sets subsequent events in motion. Later, when his daughter is returned, Chryses will offer a second prayer to end the pestilence.

Chryses's oration to Apollo is one of the most celebrated literary prayers and among the clearest representations of prayer in action—delivered in response to a specific situation and directed toward the fulfillment of specific ends. One may chart a direct link from Chryses's grievance and purposeful discourse to a material outcome of an answered prayer. In addition, one cannot fail to notice a sharp contrast between Chryses's unsuccessful demand to Agamemnon, a powerful figure with whom Chryses has no relation, and his successful appeal to Apollo, an even more powerful figure with whom he is related as priest to patron. It is this prior relationship that Chryses draws upon to persuade Apollo. Indeed, his prayer is entirely invested in establishing in the present the substance of that prior relationship.

In his mission to the Greeks, Chryses communicates that he is not to be trifled with. He openly bears insignia of his Apollonian priesthood and pointedly reminds his audience that they cannot expect to gain the support of Zeus and other Olympians in their cause against Troy if they offend Apollo. To disrespect Chryses is to disrespect Apollo. As if recognizing the relationship of priest to divine patron, the Greek forces cheer Chryses's logic and his cause—all, that is, except Agamemnon. But, in equating Apollo's arrows with his own tears, Chryses effectively makes Apollo his instrument. Indeed, he is as effective in addressing a divine audience as he is ineffective in addressing a human one. Clearly, Chryses knows how to approach and move a god.

Chryses's prayer is typical of classical petition in its three-part structure of address: epithets that recognize a particular manifestation of a god; argument for why a request should be granted; and the request itself.[1] Andrew M. Miller identifies the second section of the prayer as a *hypomnesis*, a "reminder" in which the relationship between beseecher and beseeched serves as explicit warrant. Typically, this reminder assumes an "if ever . . . then" form of reasoning to articulate prior obligations or future benefits as justification for a particular entreaty. (2). Kevin Crotty observes that such arguments do not arouse pity or appeal to justice, as they might in other contexts, but instead emphasize ongoing relationships and reciprocity (95).[2] In contrast to contemporary perspectives that question the propriety of bargaining with God or appealing to divine beings with outright flattery, nothing here suggests prayer should *not* be rhetorical in a strategic sense or should not demonstrably negotiate with heavenly powers. To the contrary, Chryses understands that prayer is a *techné*, a means for finding leverage with the divine powers. Indeed, Chryses would not *be* a priest if he lacked skill in appealing to Apollo. His prayer further underscores that individual utterances do not exist in a vacuum but arise out of established relationships between prayer's human speakers and divine audiences.

This chapter examines prayer as a *scene of address*, a term I draw from Burke's *Grammar of Motives*, where *scene* refers to dynamic relations among agents in discourse, and from his *Rhetoric of Motives*, where Burke claims rhetoric is concerned with "the *persuasive* aspects of language, the function of language as *addressed*, as direct or roundabout appeal to real or ideal audiences, without or within" (43–44, emphasis in original).[3] This encompassing statement zeroes in on the core feature of discourse—its character as address in all modes, even those of self-persuasion or magic. Indeed, Burke's insights into the scope and significance of rhetoric as address can lead us to better understand the operations of address in its many forms, some effectively hidden even from their performers within modes other than the vocative.[4] This dimension of appeal to a range of audiences, varying in proximity, accessibility, tangibility, and resemblance to rhetors, is a necessary starting place for a rhetoric of prayer. For it is in prayer, I argue, that the rhetorical character of discourse as address is most sharply rendered.

If anything characterizes a rhetorical approach to prayer, it is that prayer is a relationship realized symbolically in discourse. As address, prayer is conceived primarily in the modality of speech, of saying something to someone. Yet prayer is not restricted to verbal communication only, even when it is conceived in words. At one level, prayer's character as address seems beyond argument. Although, for most of us, prayer is discourse directed toward divine beings, for others, it may not require a divine audience. For them, prayer may be an experience of relationship or an elevated state of consciousness. Similarly, prayer may be identified as a mode of introspection (looking inward) rather than interpersonal communication (speaking outward).

Prayer may be understood as a form of what Michel Foucault calls "technologies of the self" (16). Foucault recognizes the existence of certain tools that allow for self-constitution and self-care and that enable "individuals to effect by their own means or with the help of others a certain number of operations on their own bodies and souls, thoughts, conduct, and way of being, to transform themselves to attain a certain state of happiness, purity, wisdom, perfection, or immortality" (18).[5] These tools operate in tandem with other technologies of production, sign systems, and power in a "matrix of practical reason" (18). Prayer is undeniably a technology or mix of such technologies, as are the domains of religion and philosophy more broadly. Prayer is a particular effort toward care and constitution of the self, individual and collective, whose operations are structured as dialogical relations.[6]

Prayer may also be understood as a receptive act of listening: as humans striving to be *addressed by*, rather than to address, a divine audience. Indeed, many modes of meditation, including "centering prayer," are figured as active listening.[7] In some forms, prayer is a mystical process that transcends communication in speech for an experience of communion with the divine in *silence* because the active self must be stilled in anticipation of spiritual fusion with the divine. Silence is thus conceived as a mode of address that perfects speech. Such reconfigurations of verbal prayer are possible to the extent that a scene of address may be realized in the act as opposed to the content of discursive relations, which, in turn, are abstractly imagined. Thus certain practices of prayer are conceived as a negation rather than a perfection of address. This is achieved by purging thought to reach a state of bliss. Although differently imagined, these negative realizations of a scene of prayer are quite close operationally to their positive counterparts in that both involve departure from articulate speech, whether in transcendence or retreat.

Such conceptual frames for prayer are ultimately grounded in a scene of address. Even in the closely related act of affirmation, the self is figured as an audience capable of responding to an address from the speaker.[8] In meditative prayer, both silent reception and self-emptying strive to correct defects in the communicative scene of "ordinary" spoken discourse, perceived to have succumbed to self-absorption or presumption or to be lacking either in proper regard for the activity of prayer or in proper reverence of its audience. Indeed, certain modes of prayer reflect deep concern about either the limitations of language as a reliable instrument of communication or the deficiencies of those who wield this instrument. Because prayer is imagined with respect to some divine audience dramatically configured as witness, I contend that a scene of address is fundamental to prayer, notwithstanding significant variations in how it is realized.

A scene of address distinguishes prayer from other forms of "god talk" (theology, creed, myth). Even discourse in such forms as oracular utterance or sacred scripture (as divine Word) is not prayer; these forms lack an imagined scene of encounter conceived as a human response to the divine. Prayer is *asymmetric* (one-way) discourse that yet unfolds within a scene of *dialogic* (two-way) encounter. Even when imagined as a dialogic encounter, prayer's asymmetry remains crucial to its operational logic. Whether conceived as speaking, listening, visualizing, or some other mode, prayer is the human side of any human-divine encounter.

Equally crucial for prayer, then, is the human person as instrument of performance. The *embodied* nature of prayer is evident in its multiple nondiscursive modes, likewise conceived in terms of address. That is to say, prayer is manifested in gesture, dance, and other movement and in ritual action involving candles, water, beads, and the like as media to extend the physical body. These, too, are acts of address when they augment speech or substitute for it. A lit candle, for example, is a synecdoche of a mental or verbal act, made visible as light and extended in time. In a devotional setting, a candle corroborates the reverential stance of its sponsor. As a material seconding of a verbal act, a candle may "speak" with a clarity and purity that words do not possess.

As these complexities of mode indicate, a scene of address in prayer is conceptualized in verbal terms, yet realized in multiple symbolic ways. Address is performance—a phenomenon of *act*, in dramatistic terms. The corresponding motive of *scene* refers to the ground on which communication occurs. Such ground is productively understood in terms of the respective identities of human and divine beings in relationship that makes communication possible. Crucially, these respective identities involve a shared capacity for language realized in the act of address. Thus is prayer imagined as possible, even obligatory, despite radical differences in the nature of human and divine beings. Divine beings are both like and unlike human beings in their capacities for discourse. However, the capacity to be *addressed* is the crucial projection of the human onto the divine. To characterize prayer as a scene of address, then, is to be concerned with the conditions that allow for discourse to be heard.

Thus I contend that prayer is a phenomenon of address—an activity conceived as speech notwithstanding its ready extension into other modes. Although this is hardly surprising, given how deeply orality figures in folk theories of prayer, this oral dimension must nonetheless be emphasized. For, as address, prayer is a phenomenon of *utterance*, a unit of speech Mikhail Bakhtin argues is fundamental to discourse. Utterance is discourse that takes place in the present and lends itself to an experience of *presence*. Whether textual, bodily, or even digital in manifestation, prayer is discourse experienced in the immediacy of speech. Before taking up these concerns, however, let us consider a radically different approach to prayer as an illuminating contrast to the rhetorical account offered here, one that clarifies the stakes involved in adopting a perspective centered in notions of address, hearing, and presence.

Healing Words: An Antirhetoric of Prayer

In one of many recently published books fusing science with spirituality, Larry Dossey offers a simple claim: for reasons not fully understood, prayer is instrumental in restoring and maintaining physical health.[9] This assertion is neither surprising nor controversial in itself. Many people believe that a hopeful attitude in the face of adversity, including challenges to health, can contribute to a positive outcome. Many further believe in prayer as a potent, even miraculous, force in such situations. One need not profess a belief in God to believe in the power of prayer.

But *Healing Words* does not claim that we can ask a divine being to hear our prayer, confident it will be answered. Rather, Dossey urges his readers to believe that prayer itself directly and instrumentally affects health, whether we pray or others pray *for* us. Throughout his book, Dossey (a physician who champions alternative medicine) cites studies demonstrating both that prayer cures diseases and stimulates growth in animals, plants, and even yeast and that positive results are often obtained when prayer's human beneficiaries are unaware they are being prayed for. These outcomes hold even when—a point crucial to Dossey—prayer's beneficiaries are at great physical distance from the scene of prayer. He further maintains that it does not matter to whom one prays, only *that* one prays. The activity itself produces positive outcomes. Perhaps his most astonishing claim is that prayer—a "nonlocal" activity (whose effects are not "confined to the present or the future"—"may affect *past* events, even though they seem already to have taken place" (8, emphasis added).

Dossey's concept of prayer requires no mediator for its intended effects. Indeed, he insists that prayer works not because divine agents "bend an ear" to human pleas but because prayer, as a form of thought or energy, cooperates with the material world as a transformative agency. Prayerful thought need not even entail conscious activity: unconscious, even "dream," prayer is possible. Dossey goes so far as to propose that an attitude of "prayerfulness" is just as effective as discrete acts of prayer—if not more so. He further contends that less specific intentions for a positive outcome may prove more successful than specific ones.

Dossey recognizes his perspective is at odds with theistic models of prayer appealing to gods as personal beings, as Chryses does in his prayer to Apollo. Indeed, mixing parapsychology, Jungian metaphysics, and experimental science, *Healing Words* has little to do with any conventional understanding of prayer. It stands out in the present context for its extraordinary and contrastive positions with respect to prayer as a mode of rhetorical action. Dossey considers his view of prayer a distinct advance over traditional, "dualistic" views that have prayer direct language to a being "installed outside us, usually high above, as if in stationary orbit, functioning as a sort of master communications satellite" (7).

> The old biblically based views of prayer, which are still largely in vogue, were developed when a view of the world was in place that is now antiquated and incomplete. In this century our fundamental ideas about how the universe works have changed. We have redefined our ideas about the nature of space, time, energy, and causation. These bear little resemblance to the views that dominated human thought for millennia in the West, and that shaped our concepts of prayer. In addition, our basic ideas of the structure and function of the human psyche have been radically transformed and continue to evolve. If our world view has changed, perhaps we should also reevaluate our views of the nature of prayer. (7)

Dossey may well be right that our understanding of nature, including our own, has greatly changed and that epistemologies and ontologies have changed in ways that challenge long-held notions of prayer. Indeed, many no longer hold with confidence traditional theories of divine action. Even so, he greatly overstates the degree to which cognitive revolutions have fundamentally changed how we experience the world.

What Dossey imprecisely calls "biblically based views" persist *not* because they depend on a particular cosmology but because they manifest basic patterns of experience with other persons. These views are not so much "biblically based" as they are a perennial understanding of our world. The anthropomorphic qualities prayer projects upon divine beings are regularly perceived in the operations of the physical world. What we now describe as inanimate forces of wind and water were once imagined to possess animate properties of consciousness and will—and they still are when we "forget" to think otherwise.

Dossey distorts traditional notions of prayer beyond recognition. Though he allows for prayers to be addressed to "the Absolute, God, Goddess, Tao, Brahman, Allah, however the Ultimate may be conceived," his model denies real agency to these beings (70). For Dossey, it hardly matters which personification or abstraction one chooses since those prayed to are merely a focus for the energy of thought. In rescuing prayer from the supernatural, he replaces traditional notions of prayer as addressed discourse with notions of agency centered in the mind. This mind, however, is not "localized within an individual brain or body, or confined to the present moment," but a mind "spread through space and time" (43). Capitalizing on contemporary trends in spirituality to give paranormal "science" a religious veneer, Dossey makes the idea of prayer all but unrecognizable. His account of prayer as "mental action at a distance" is a nearly perfect foil for prayer as a rhetoric of symbolic action. What he brackets off as mere ornament is precisely what is most interesting about prayer: its strategic coaxing of the divine into cooperation with the human. For Dossey, a scene of address to divine audiences is the figurative device of apostrophe. But presumptions of anthropomorphism, insofar as they reify notions of our human rhetorical potential, are precisely what gives prayer its dynamism. Dossey's claim that ancient cosmologies and psychologies have been superseded by modern belief systems is flatly wrong. It is more accurate to say that modern science, invested in impersonal forces and inexorable laws of cause and effect, shares the stage with older cosmologies in which otherworldly agents are active in human affairs. It is in notions of the personal—human qualities shared with the divine—that our conceptions of prayer are situated. In figurative terms, prayer *is* personification.

Healing Words would preserve prayer's efficacy, operating upon or cooperating with the physical world, without preserving its rhetorical character as discourse interacting with like-minded others. In presenting prayer as direct mental action, Dossey elevates thought over language and agents; in a word, he offers not prayer but magic. And a strange sort of magic at that—assigning agency to thought itself: things are what we think they are. Magic traditionally focuses on finding the right language and the right actions to harness natural powers. Dossey's science of mind eliminates the need for rhetorical craft. But prayer's use of language to move an audience, rather than to directly operate upon persons and objects, is what fundamentally distinguishes prayer from magic. In the end, *Healing Words* offers neither religion nor science, neither prayer nor magic, but only "wishcraft."

In "The Philosophy of Literary Form," Kenneth Burke maintains that "it is difficult to keep the magical decree and the religious petition totally distinct. Though the distinction between the coercive command and the conducive request is clear enough in the extremes, there are many borderline cases" (*PLF* 5). A rhetoric of prayer begins in recognition of this principle. As Burke later observes in *The Rhetoric of Motives*, magic is best understood as proto-rhetoric, not primitive science. Magic, like rhetoric, is a thoroughly socialized practice. In distinguishing between the two, Burke arrives at his most important characterization of rhetoric: "the use of language as a symbolic means for inducing cooperation in beings that by nature respond to symbols" (*RM* 43). This definition is a striking contrast to Dossey's antirhetorical account of prayer as direct mental action, which only serves to suppress prayer's inherently social character. Indeed, Dossey's conception of prayer recognizes nothing of prayer's social character as a language of courtship or intimacy; it ignores the ramifications of this character in the full range of practices coming under the heading of "prayer." By contrast, Burke recognizes that a literary or religious (symbolic, personal, agent-centered) account as opposed to a scientific (material, impersonal, agency-centered) account of "action at a distance" is the most accurate and satisfying frame for understanding human cooperation with the cosmos. This is the realm of rhetoric. Burke's encompassing definition anticipates prayer in its provocative reference to "beings that by nature respond to symbols."

Prayer, then, is not an exceptional mode of rhetorical action but arguably its epitome: it is discourse at its most rhetorical in engaging divine beings. Of course, some might assign prayer to a category error—an exuberant extension of the range of "beings that by nature respond to symbols." Whatever one thinks about that, what must not be lost sight of is that prayer's symbolic operations involve multiple agents in discursive relationship, not merely the material agency of thought or language.

Rather than redefine prayer, I argue that prayer is best understood in conventional terms: the expression of symbolically mediated relationships between the human and the divine.[10] Without question, the projection of human qualities onto the divine is challenged by shifting paradigms of consciousness and causation. Even so, our basic ways of apprehending the world have not changed profoundly. What is necessary, therefore, as I claim in the introduction, is to recover prayer through careful rearticulation of what this discourse makes possible in human communities, for what roles prayer has played historically, it plays still.

Finally, it must be emphasized, contra Dossey, that a rhetoric of prayer is *not* oriented to empirical measures of efficacy. Rhetoric remains entirely on the inventional side of prayer's overtures and declines to read signs of miraculous cures, the retreat of armies, or the avoidance of fatal accidents as evidence, one way or the other, of prayer's success. A rhetoric of prayer begins—and ends—with the *character* of the discursive relationships human beings may have with divine beings (and through those relationships with other human beings). Prayer is thus grounded in a motive of scene.

Prayer as Conceptual and Verbal Scene of Address

Who, exactly, are present when prayer occurs? This question proves most important in considering prayer as rhetorical activity. In any drama, a scene is understood with respect to the characters present to one another and to an audience. Dramatic acts unfold in explicit terms from the relationships implicit between characters. When considering the many variations in prayer's performative contexts, then, questions of *who* are present in any scene and of *how* they are present to one another are especially significant. To approach prayer from the motive of scene, some representative moment in a larger unfolding drama, is to draw out prayer's character as a strategic response to an encompassing situation. As scene, prayer attends to the ground on which discursive relationships between prayer's speakers and audiences are conceived, constructed, and articulated.

This scene of address may be observed in Chryses's prayer to Apollo, which is also a scene of *recognition*: when the prayer is performed, it is crucial that Apollo know he is known by Chryses. Indeed, it is more important that Chryses stress his ongoing relationship with Apollo than that he specify the grievances that motivate his prayer. In Chryses's prayer, and in prayer more generally, conditions of relationship that justify prayer become foregrounded in the act of address. As a moment in an ongoing drama, a prayer responds to a situation, but its function is to frame this situation anew in the immediacy of discourse. In performing this function, prayer is address in a double sense: it addresses both a specific audience and a specific situation—it must articulate its situation accurately and in language addressed to an appropriate audience.

Finally, an emphasis on scene underscores the richness of prayer as performance before *multiple* audiences. Indeed, the distinction between audience and addressee is significant. Prayer makes explicit the relations that exist between speaker and addressee, while avoiding complicated matters of audience. There are substantial differences between audiences that figure as addressees and audiences that figure in prayer's performance. To be clear, prayer is a complex auditory space in which a range of audiences, human (including the self) and divine, operate. Prayer's audiences—both hearers and, significantly, overhearers—can be characterized in multiple ways: primary and secondary, direct and indirect, real and ideal, actual and imaginary. Each of these binaries captures something of the psychological, phenomenological, and rhetorical character of address. The risk in misunderstanding prayer is to proceed with too simple a model of audience and, hence, of prayer's performative possibilities.

Even in the contexts of individual or private prayer, an audience of self is positioned as an overhearer. So significant is this function of overhearing that it is possible to read prayer as an appeal to self performed indirectly through the audience function afforded by the divine addressee. Yet either to reduce prayer to an act of talking to oneself or to disregard the dimension of self-address as immaterial in these contexts is to unduly simplify prayer. More complex still are the performative contexts of congregational and public prayer, where primary, secondary, and even tertiary audiences may figure in as performers pray with, for, before, and even at others. A rhetorical analysis of any prayer must account for these various audiences in complex relation to prayer's addressees. Before undertaking such an analysis, however, we need to further consider prayer's primary conceptual scene as involving human speakers and divine addressees.

The Realm of Divine Beings

A scene of address is both a conceptual and a performative space. The conceptual space authorizes what may be said in prayer. Though this will differ with different situations, broadly similar relationships inform a scene of prayer across its distinct settings: the devil may be in the details, but the divine in prayer is in the general.

This is not to claim that all divine beings are essentially the same or even alike beneath a profusion of names and attributes. Considering the multiplicity of divinities addressed in prayer, from the personal and household gods and totemic spirits of tribes to the various gods and goddesses of polytheism and the God of monotheism, it cannot be claimed that divine beings are all the same. If anything, *no* divine being has an entirely stable identity across even a limited range of significations. Those who profess beliefs in the same divine beings imagine and experience them differently to the point of profound disagreement over what those divine beings are like. That said, the conceptual variety of divine beings within prayer is far less than the conceptual variety *beyond* prayer. The gods of prayer are not identical with the gods of our many theologies. Yet, despite the many beings who may be addressed in prayer, only certain things may be said to them in prayer

As described in chapter 1, prayer can be characterized generically as a repertoire of basic speech acts such as petition or praise. Broad similarity in *function* justifies recognizing prayer across multiple contexts as well as cultures. Prayer involves a similar bundle of acts performed with respect to different addressees and is distinguishable from other acts less by its particular addressees than by how its acts are performed. A petition to Zeus for a favorable outcome in war, a hymn to the Virgin Mary as a paragon of virtue, a memorial act of ancestor worship—these acts are not prayer simply because otherworldly audiences are addressed. These acts are prayer because divine beings are addressed *as if* they were human. This "as if" character does not erase a divide between human and divine beings. Rather, it makes a dotted line of a solid one in recognizing and overcoming a divide whose existence otherwise makes communication impossible. This "as if" dimension endows divine beings with the capacity to be addressed as an *ideal* audience. So fundamental is the assumption that divine addressees are ideal audiences that it is invisible as prayer's central premise. Indeed, its invisibility, a case of hiding in plain sight, suggests that prayer is not only an encounter with divine beings through language but also a significant encounter with language itself.

To be clear, what distinguishes prayer from other acts of address is precisely an "as if" quality that makes for consciously stylized address. In other words, prayer's analogical character, which is akin to, yet not identical with, other discourse, is present even in the most normalized of contexts. Indeed, an insistent normalizing stance—for example, a claim that prayer is "just" conversation between intimates—may be emphasized in order to bridge an ontological divide between prayer's agents, somewhat like the use of forced informality to overcome a social divide between persons of different stations.

To better understand prayer as the performative "other" to ordinary discourse, it is helpful to place it alongside a continuum of scenarios from "straightforward" extensions of ordinary discourse (the way we communicate with our pets) to consciously figurative appeals (the way we exhort natural or man-made objects to cooperate). More ambiguous are forms of apostrophe in such activities as singing anthems to abstractions or pledging allegiance to avatars of nationhood; these presumably secular forms of address strongly resemble religious acts of prayer.

Of course, prayer is not at all like our communication with animals, not simply because we are in a position of social and linguistic superiority to them, but also because symbolic interaction with animals is a natural extension of ordinary discourse. Closer to prayer, perhaps, is our discourse with plants in appreciation of their beauty or to encourage their flourishing. Both occur at one remove from ordinary communication; at some level, we remain aware of the fiction. Likewise, exhorting a car engine to start on a winter morning resembles prayer's "as if" character as an optative appeal. Neither of these scenarios is equivalent to prayer, but each takes its place on a continuum from most natural to most conceptually strange acts of communication.

In prayer, beings conceived as distinctly other are yet conceived as not *wholly* other. Were it not for profound differences in power between human and divine beings, there would be no need for prayer. At the same time, were human and divine beings not *consubstantial* at some level, there would be no possibility of prayer. My use of "consubstantial" here echoes Burke's account of rhetoric as identification through "shared substance" (*RM* 20–21). The assumption of linguistic consubstantiality between human speakers and divine addressees is fundamental to prayer, which is possible only because human speakers and divine audiences stand upon shared linguistic ground.

That said, the linguistic capacities of human and divine beings do not entirely correspond. Prayer projects linguistic capacities onto divine beings but does so selectively. Although divine beings may be said to "speak" our language, they do not possess language the way human beings do. The crucial point is that they "hear" language addressed to them. Divine beings do not speak (or hear) any particular human language. Their possession of language is more comprehensive and conceptual. In contrast to human beings, divine beings do not learn language or *a* language.

Mythological or religious accounts of communication between human and divine beings explain how a common linguistic ground comes to be. In the book of Genesis, human beings are said to be created in the "image" and "likeness" of God (1:26), an identification imagined as mutual intelligibility. Of course, strictly secular accounts might reverse the terms to claim divine beings possess language because they are created in *human* likeness. In whichever direction the capacity for language can be said to flow, the presumption of linguistic consubstantiality in address to the divine is paramount. If divine beings exist, they "speak" our language and may be addressed.

Although, in principle, divine beings may always be appealed to, in some cases they do not hear the prayers addressed to them. If human speakers must pay attention in prayer, they must also gain the attention of their divine addressees. Divine beings may be prayed to inattentively or otherwise improperly. Yet failure in prayer occurs not because divine beings are unable to understand. The burden remains on human beings to make themselves understood. An ideal scene of communication may impose additional constraints on performance in the use of specialized languages for prayer in certain contexts or the restriction of prayer to socially sanctioned mediators such as priests or shamans. Despite exacting constraints for proper prayer, the capacity of divine beings to be addressed remains axiomatic.

An exception that proves the rule are those otherworldly entities in the form of monsters, aliens, demons, and such imagined as falling outside the circle of language, in whole or in part. To these unearthly beings, linguistic appeals fail. Inaccessible through speech, they inhabit our fantasies and nightmares. They are never addressed in prayer because their lack of linguistic consubstantiality makes genuine communication impossible. Although they cannot be prayed to, they may yet be appeased or repelled by language conceived as a more powerful force. The folk belief that a crucifix will ward off a vampire is an instance of a symbolic, but nonlinguistic, appeal—a crude form of address. As examples of otherworldly, but also not divine, beings underscore, it is only beings who share fully our linguistic nature, possessing these capacities more perfectly than we do, who are imagined as realistic audiences for prayer.

Stated simply, divine beings are linguistically consubstantial with human beings *because* human beings desire to address them. A discovery that prayer is indeed possible makes persuasion on the basis of shared interests imaginable. Linguistic consubstantiality thus serves as a compelling warrant for rhetorical agency, not just as a necessary precondition for communication. To speak another's language is already to exercise some claim over that other, to already be in relationship.

We do not posit the existence of divine beings only to claim that they are beyond the reach of human address. Indeed, their responsiveness to linguistic appeal trumps even their existence since it is possible to experience relationships with beings we do not, strictly speaking, believe in. To allow for this possibility, however, is to stand on a slippery slope that leads to denying the existence of divine beings altogether. Such a move reduces prayer to apostrophe, address as figurative convention. Yet such reduction is not inevitable, for this slope may also allow us to slip *upward* from imaginative acts of address to the recognition of divine beings as real beyond all imagining. This is to say that divine beings are not first posited, then addressed. They are experienced *through* address and discovered to be not mere addressees but also audiences.

We come, then, to what I argue is prayer's abiding concern as a meta-rhetorical practice: what it means to be an audience. Addressees as audiences are always more or less figurative constructions that speakers project onto the world. The fictiveness of an audience is neither more nor less true in prayer than in other rhetorical acts. The crucial concern of prayer, I contend, is that its addressees be real audiences, by which I mean beings that may be addressed as if they were real. Implicit in this concern is recognition that addressing a *real* audience and not a fictive construction is a profoundly challenging act. This concern is manifested in a desire to encounter addressees beyond their names or to discover ever better names. When particular scenes of address have lost their resonance, new scenes of address may arise in their place.

This reading of prayer is consonant with Burke's characterization of rhetoric as a capacity "not rooted in any past condition of human society [but] in an essential function of language itself, a function that is wholly realistic, and is continually born anew; the use of language as a symbolic means of inducing cooperation in beings that by nature respond to symbols" (*RM* 43). The first part of this statement is as relevant to the present discussion as the second, already discussed part. If prayer *is* rhetoric, its functions are coextensive with our capacities for communication generally. No evolutionary stage of cognition or social development, rhetoric is the very texture of discourse. Approached from this perspective, prayer is less a relic of another era and more a normative practice for our constitution as social beings. Considering that prayer perfects socialization, the more interesting issue is not why prayer remains but why its objects of address have experienced radical revaluation in the modern era. Burke claims that prayer goes underground, becoming secularized in new outlets, objects of address, and hierarchical relations. The essential functions of prayer remain because we are programmed as social beings endowed with language to plead, curse, applaud, pledge fidelity, assert obligation, and other relational acts manifested in prayer.

Admittedly, such a reading of prayer risks making divinity into a purely technical concept, a mere function of a scene of address. In his *Rhetoric of Motives*, Burke speaks of "the ultimate rhetorical motive of *homo dialecticus*," in which "prayer, as pure beseechment, would be addressed not to an *object* (which might "answer" the prayer by providing booty) but to *the hierarchic principle itself*, where the answer is implicit in the address" (276, emphasis in original). This view takes address to its logical end. In prayer, that end is realized in mystical communion with the divine. Practically speaking, no pure prayer of this kind exists because prayer is not a one-way principle of projection. It is address to and apprehension of the real. In other words, what is addressed in prayer is not nothing before it is addressed. Beneath abstraction and figuration is the real, to be encountered in dialogic terms. Another way to say this is that in prayer the audience answers back, even if the character of that response is open to interpretation.

It seems strange to maintain that prayer is concerned with the real when divine beings are clothed in such heavy figurative garb. Yet, prayer insists, the materiality of being is not finally separable from the spirituality of being. To become prayerful objects of address, otherworldly beings (Earth and Sun, the spirit of a city, the concept of eros, the Creator God) precede their identification as objects of address. At the same time, only in being addressed as apprehensions of the real do prayer's audiences become divine. This is to say that conceptions of divine beings are experienced in symbolic relationship. Less obviously, divine beings are implicated in experiences with language as a means of address. Burke's insight into the "*the hierarchic principle itself*" can be read in this context of prayer as recognition that language is itself a motive of relationship, expressible as an *agency-scene* relation (or *agency-agent* relation since the scene is the relation between agents). Language constructs a circle of human and divine audiences responsive to symbolic appeals. Broadening the circle to include the divine occurs naturally enough, for it is through instruments of language, zealously applied, that we rhetorically engage the real.

Language necessarily intervenes between rhetors and audiences—as aid but also as impediment. (At times, one sees through the language window; at other times, one sees *only* the window.) This is to say that prayer is both an encounter with the real *through* language as well as an encounter *with* language as a means for communicating with the real. Few discursive acts provoke as much awareness of or anxiety about their medium as prayer does.

On Hearing and Being Heard

The expectation that one will be heard is the most common of prayer's commonplaces. On one side a speaker and on the other side an audience, brought into relationship through *utterance*: this is the discursive equation. Marking prayer as "utterance" recognizes the dialogic, hence social dimensions of discourse that Mikhail Bakhtin locates in "addressivity," which he characterizes as the "quality of being directed toward someone" ("Speech Genres" 95).[11] For Bakhtin, addressivity is an "essential (constitutive) marker of the utterance" (95). This notion, strikingly similar to Burke's location of rhetoric in acts of address, is also notable for its emphasis on audience and therefore on hearing.

Owing to the dialogic nature of discourse, prayer is grounded in scenes of reception as the complements to scenes of address. As previously noted, in some traditions, prayer is conceived as realizing its potential in practices of reception whose purpose is to transform human agents into both better speakers and better listeners. Indeed, prayer merits consideration for its emphasis on listening, the receptive opening of self to another, as a profound rhetorical art. Outside prayer, the role of listening in rhetoric has long been subordinated to speaking.

This is no longer the case, however. In his final critical work, *The Rhetoric of Rhetoric*, Wayne Booth calls for a "listening rhetoric" that would manifest a commitment to genuine dialogue. Krista Ratcliffe similarly delineates such possibilities in *Rhetorical Listening*, identifying "rhetorical listening as a trope of interpretive invention" open to difference (25). Ratcliffe acknowledges a debt to theater scholar Alice Rayner, who articulates an *audience*'s obligations to performance. For Rayner, audience is "not a thing or a person but an act" (20). Specifically, an audience grants to any performance a hearing. Echoing François Lyotard, Rayner recognizes that what an audience ultimately grants is *legitimacy* "through the ability to donate to the performer both presence and judgement: this donation is an ethics of relation not simply of power over, for it returns the speaker to itself with a difference" (21).[12] The notion of returning speakers to themselves "with a difference" is especially insightful in that performance is fraught with challenge. As a scene of address, prayer opens speakers and audiences to new possibilities, including the real possibility that performance will be misheard—or go unheard.

As primarily an auditory phenomenon, prayer is attentive to notions of both proximity and presence since in oral communication speakers must be sufficiently near auditors to be heard. As Walter Ong observes in *The Presence of the Word*: "Sound and hearing have a special relationship to our sense of presence. When we speak of a presence in its fullest sense—the presence which we experience in the case of another human being, which another person exercises on us, and which no object or no living being less than human can exercise—we speak of something that surrounds us, in which we are situated. I am in his presence, we say, not in front of his presence. Being in is what we experience in a world of sound" (130). For Ong, hearing is active engagement with the world. In much the same vein, Michael Holquist comments on Bakhtin's dialogic approach to discourse: "The world addresses us and we are alive and human to the degree that we are answerable, i.e., to the degree that we can respond to addressivity. We are responsible to the degree that we are compelled to respond, we cannot choose but to give the world an answer" (28). To hear is already to act and be acted upon.

Not surprisingly, prayer is explicitly figured as a scene of hearing: "Hear!" As an appeal to a shared linguistic ground, this act is already a complete prayer, whether expressed in a particular invocation or implied in the act of address itself. An audience for prayer, then, is not simply a suitable object of address. As Rayner contends, an audience is an addressee deemed capable of granting a hearing, that is to say, capable of being present and giving judgment. Openness, even vulnerability, to the free response of this audience is what distinguishes the address of prayer from that of apostrophe.

The latent rhetorical power manifested in scenes of address or hearing is evident in the central prayer of Judaism, the Shema (Hebrew for "hear"): "Hear, O Israel: The Lord is our God, the Lord is One" (Deut. 6:4, NIV). This first line and, indeed, the entirety of the prayer are a call to mindfulness, a call to witness the covenantal relationship between the Lord and the Jewish people. In a technical sense, the Shema is not a prayer at all, for it is addressed to *Israel*, not to the Lord. Although not the addressee, the Lord is nonetheless positioned as an indirect but intended audience of this appeal. Yet the Shema is most obviously a prayer. In performative terms, it calls into presence a scene of address between the human and the divine. As Ong astutely recognizes in *The Presence of the Word*, hearing calls upon the deepest part of ourselves as persons and communities. Hearing connotes obedience, for to hear *is* to obey (as indicated by *obey*'s Latin root *oboedire*, to listen). Linguist Eve Sweetser, in *From Etymology to Pragmatics*, similarly connects hearing in physical terms to notions of responsiveness. Noting that this semantic link is found in virtually all languages and may be a universal, Sweetser remarks that "it is natural that physical auditory reception should be linked with heedfulness and internal 'receptivity' . . . and to obedience" (41).

What, then, does it mean to hear in prayer, if hearing is the reciprocal of addressing? The act of hearing in prayer productively shuttles between metaphorical and material senses. Beneath all prayer is a prayer for hearing. Yet a necessary divide exists between a scene of address and a scene of hearing. This is precisely the gap prayer is devoted to closing. The example of Chyrses's prayer to Apollo is one in which prayer's felicity conditions have all been met.[13] Here a prayer addressed is a prayer both heard and answered. Yet prayer is more complicated than this: to pray is to confront failure as much as it is to encounter success. As I have suggested, prayer can go wrong in multiple ways. Unless its felicity conditions are met, prayer remains unheard.

On the other hand, it is *extra*-rhetorical to consider prayer from the vantage point of Chryses's prayer, which is answered in spectacular fashion and thus has been well delivered. Rather than focus on answered prayer as a measure of rhetorical success, I conclude this analysis by proposing that a successful prayer is one that has been *heard*.

To say that a prayer "has been heard" is still to consider this act from the perspective of its performer. Here the passive voice is significant. For a prayer to have been heard, it must fulfill ethical demands of address implicit in the conditions of prayer's scene: mutual intelligibility and responsiveness. These conditions are manifested in dialogic exchange. As the human side of this exchange, address aspires to represent the ethical dimensions of that scene. It does so at the level of *character*, for it must recognize who, precisely, are in this scene. The performative challenge of prayer is to discover one's character within this scene and to remain in character before the other whom one addresses. In a phenomenological sense, prayer is a discovery of whom one stands before in a scene of address and who one is in standing. Only through such a dialectic of address to the other and apprehension of the other is prayer an experience of being heard.

This experience of being heard in prayer begins in the implicit hope that one *may* be heard, provided one prays correctly and to the right audience. For no one prays in the certain belief that the exercise is either futile or pro forma. A scene of prayer is entered when speakers find themselves performing an address that seeks to apprehend the real. The beings addressed in prayer, from Apollo to Saint Anthony to the avatars of Vishnu, are those about whom an experience of discursive relationship is conceived as possible. Every culture and individual differently determines the horizon of possibility, including certain audiences for prayer and excluding others. This determination is grounded in anticipation of being heard: the prayer "If I pray to you, in this way, I will be heard" underwrites all other prayer.

Bakhtin's concept of the "superaddressee" as an implicit third party to a dialogic exchange is one way to characterize in personal terms what I have defined in operational terms as an experience of being heard: "The author of the utterance, with a greater or lesser awareness, presupposes a higher superaddressee (third), whose absolutely just responsive understanding is presumed, either in some metaphysical distance or in distant historical time (the loophole addressee). In various ages and with various understandings of the world, this superaddressee and his ideally true responsive understanding assume various ideological expression" ("Problem of the Text" 126). This third-party superaddressee exists in the socialized minds of interlocutors and sits in judgment over both speaker and second-party addressee. In prayer, it is that judgment which renders a verdict of having been heard, that is to say, of having made a good prayer. Bakhtin explains that the superaddressee is "a constitutive aspect of the whole utterance," a characterization that suggests a superaddressee above is related to the base below in a dialogic or trialogic relationship (127).[14]

Indeed, the capacity of performers to hear themselves in prayer is crucial. One can even claim that prayer *is* the experience of hearing oneself in an act of address, though this is not the same as addressing oneself indirectly. In this sense, hearing connotes responsiveness to discursive appeals, including one's own. Prayer depends on being conscious of what one is saying in an act of address such that one makes oneself present within the scene and ethically responsive to the scene.

Returning a final time to Chryses's prayer to Apollo: a crucial aspect of the persuasive force Chryses is able to wield in his prayer is Apollo's need to protect his reputation as a god to be feared and respected. Much is at stake in this event by which his priest is so publicly humiliated. Not only do Chryses and Apollo have a special relationship as priest and patron; this relationship is also widely known. Protecting one's reputation is a factor unique neither to the classical era nor to a polytheistic framework. The larger point is that Chryses's private prayer occurs within a broader framework in which prayer is shaped by a common vision. Prayer involves a social self, one located in a complex auditory space where hearing, overhearing, and being heard form an experiential bundle, one bound with social norms of, in Rayner's words, "presence and judgement" (21). We judge prayer's aptness and potential effectiveness by criteria drawn from social norms for discourse. What persuades others, what persuades us, persuades prayer's addressees as well. Indeed, absent shared norms or concerns about being overheard by others, the performance of prayer quickly descends into monologue, as if speaking before a mirror. And monologue is *failed* prayer, prayer that has lost, or has never found, an audience.

The range of commitment to the force of utterance in prayer will certainly vary, from an attitude of privilege ("I will be heard"), to confidence ("I know I will be heard"), to desperation ("O God, I hope you can hear me"), and even to skepticism ("I'm not sure you are listening, but . . ."). So long as it retains awareness of its character of address, it remains prayer. As Bakhtin's colleague Valentin Voloshinov writes:

Word is a two-sided act. It is determined equally by whose word it is and for whom it is meant. As word, it is precisely the product of the reciprocal relationship between speaker and listener, addresser and addressee. Each and every word expresses the "one" in relation to the "other." I give myself verbal shape from another's point of view, ultimately, from the point of view of the community to which I belong. A word is a bridge thrown between myself and another. If one end of the bridge depends on me, then the other depends on my addressee. A word is territory shared by both addresser and addressee, by the speaker and his interlocutor. (85–86)

This character of prayer as a scene of address, "territory shared by both addresser and addressee," is one that calls upon the self in relation to the other even as it calls upon the other. Through address, prayer opens up to dynamic possibilities brought about by the transformative capacities of utterance. In brief, prayer changes things. Prayer calls new situations into being rather than merely ratifying existing ones. Chapter 3 considers the transformative opportunities implied in a scene of address and expressed in an act of address, under the heading of "invocations."

3

INVOCATIONS OF SPIRIT:
PRAYER AS SPEECH ACT

Prayer is characteristically a dangerous act, and dangerous rhetoric is required
to match the intent of the act. It is an awesome matter to voice one's life
before God, and our lives should therefore be awesomely uttered.

—Walter Brueggemann, *Awed to Heaven, Rooted to Earth*

The magical decree is implicit in all language; for the mere act of naming
an object or situation decrees that it is to be singled out as such-and-such
rather than as something else. Hence, I think that an attempt to eliminate
magic, in this sense, would involve us in the elimination
of vocabulary itself as a way of sizing up reality.

—Kenneth Burke, *Philosophy of Literary Form*

Prayer does not change God, but it changes the one who offers it.

—Søren Kierkegaard, *Purity of Heart Is to Will One Thing*

"Listen!" "Come!" Prayer may arguably be reduced to these exclamations. "Listen! I have something to say." "Come! Your presence is desired." The first presumes a state of mutual presence between a speaker and an audience. The second, whether performed as a demand or a request, brings into being by its very utterance a state of presence. Together, they are the pulse of prayer.

If the language of prayer tells us anything, it is that the gods come when they are called. This is the authorizing assumption behind all acts of verbal appeal to the divine. Consequently, one must be serious in using the power of language to draw the divine into human presence, and vice versa. Responsive to human speech, divine beings become present to those who call upon them. This capacity to respond is a conceptual given for the possibility of relationship. For a prayer to be heard, to be responded to, human and divine beings must first be in mutual presence. This is accomplished through invocation.

An invocation, I argue, is more than a formal salutation signaling the beginning of an address. It is a strategic act, one that pronounces the name of the divine to claim a relationship between those who call and those who are called. This strategic character is particularly evident when invocation employs amplification, hyperbole, or other elements of stylistic elevation to signal the momentous nature of summoning divine presence. Divine beings manifest the character by which they are called. Speakers summon divine beings in a particular capacity—some property or power—in naming what they address. In these acts of naming, speakers likewise implicate themselves in relationship. As speech that asserts, "We know each other," invocations spell out the identities of the invoked in relation to those who invoke.

This spelling out, which can be extended even to the casting of spells, is always present in invocation to some degree. The incantation of magic, Kenneth Burke recognizes, is cousin to the invocation of prayer: "The magical decree is implicit in all language; for the mere act of naming an object or situation decrees that it is to be singled out as such-and-such rather than as something else" (*PLF* 4). Where Burke highlights the rhetorical power inherent in acts of naming, Walter Brueggemann warns of the risks attendant to that power: "Prayer is characteristically a dangerous act, and dangerous rhetoric is required to match the intent of the act. It is an awesome matter to voice one's life before God, and our lives should therefore be awesomely uttered" (xvi). As "dangerous rhetoric," invocation articulates the situations in which prayer's speakers find themselves, but to advantage. As invocation, prayer articulates a hoped-for state of affairs, but it begins in recognition of some actual state. Prayer thus depends on knowing where one stands relative to the divine. Invocation, the rhetorical act by which such stands are characterized, invites an "Amen" to these characterizations as a prelude to possibility.

By locating prayer's performative core in invocation, rather than in petition or praise, I depart significantly from convention. In my view, as prayer's most distinctive speech act, invocation makes prayer possible; it must be understood in reciprocity with acts by which speakers bring themselves into a scene of prayer. Thus invocation is a dialectic of power and presence. Moreover, although not confined by specific markers of address, even if such markers serve as linguistic and conceptual anchors, invocation accomplishes its rhetorical work in the semantic content and pragmatic force of its particular markers.

Where chapter 2 focused on the motive of *scene*, this chapter focuses on prayer primarily as *act*, the complement to scene. In dramatistic terms, it shifts attention from a *scene-act* relation to one of *act-scene*, a reversal that can be characterized as a shift of perspective from prayer as stasis to prayer as *motion*.

The Language of Invocation

In *A Grammar of Motives*, Kenneth Burke sets out a method whereby a performative whole may be understood through its motivational elements, in particular through dramatistic relations. "The scene contains the act," Burke observes; likewise, "the scene contains the agents" (3). The scene-act and scene-agent relations frame an interpretation of any dramatic whole differently because of the elements each relates and stresses. Prayer's *scenes* are human agents in relationship with divine agents (on the basis of linguistic consubstantiality and a fundamental condition of dependence—considered more substantively in chapter 4). Prayer's *acts* realize the potential of these scenes. A symbolic act unfurls what is implicit in its scene. Prayer gives voice to scene, converting potential into kinetic energy.

To a great extent, as we have seen in the preceding chapters, prayer's context and content are one. Prayers reflexively recount speakers' relationships with their audiences, as in the following Old Testament psalm:

> I will extol you, O Lord, for you have drawn me up, and did not let my
> foes rejoice over me;
> O Lord my God, I cried to you for help, and you have healed me.
> O Lord, you brought up my soul from Sheol, restored me to life from
> among those gone down to the Pit. (Ps. 30:1–3)

This prayer of thanksgiving acknowledges deliverance from evil (especially from the gloating of enemies); it is addressed, appropriately, to the source of that deliverance. The psalm recounts past performance of prayer, emphasizing that *this* discourse is part of an unfolding drama of divine-human relations. Thus it is crucial to voice awareness of one's situation. Moreover, it is crucial to do so by addressing those agents in the relationship from which discourse arises as a form of debt paid in words of gratitude. What is true of thanksgiving is true of other speech acts. Prayer takes form as performatives ("I confess," "I praise") acknowledging situations. These performatives lend prayer the formality necessary for performing the invocation that brings a scene of mutual presence into being.

Prayer may be even more explicitly referential, as in this Zoroastrian hymn:

I address myself to thee, Ahura Mazda, to whom all worship is due. With outstretched arms and open mind and my whole heart, I greet thee in spirit. I will not turn my gaze from thee. My eyes and my ears and my mind and my heart are all lifted up to thee. Lift up thy countenance upon me and make thy face to shine upon me. Thy look sets my soul aflame. I set thy radiant face before me and a gleam of sunshine steals into the darkness of my heart, even as the light of the sun chases away the darkness and gloom of the night. Thy image is engraven in my breast. I give my all to thee. I give myself to thee, both body and soul, wholly and completely, as Zarathustra did. (Dhalla)

Here address foregrounds affect and the awe that gives rise to utterance, in effect, speaking what it performs: "I worship you. I desire you." More than the expression of feeling, prayer is feeling directed toward its proper object. And though prayer is not primarily a narrative art—few of its stories are sustained at any length—it dramatizes a scene of utterance, largely in the present. In effect, prayer says, "I say this now because of you and for what you have done." As suggested by this hymn, prayer relies on rhetorical strategies of accumulation to sustain presence and resist closure.

The continuation of Psalm 30 illustrates complexities of address that formal prayer allows:

> Sing praises to the LORD, O you his faithful ones, and give thanks to his
>   holy name.
> For his anger is but for a moment; his favor is for a lifetime.
> Weeping may linger for the night, but joy comes with the morning.
> As for me, I said in my prosperity, "I shall never be moved."
> By your favor, O LORD, you had established me as a strong mountain;
> You hid your face; I was dismayed.
> To you, O LORD, I cried, and to the LORD I made supplication:
> "What profit is there in my death, if I go down to the Pit?
> Will the dust praise you? Will it tell of your faithfulness?
> Hear, O LORD, and be gracious to me! O LORD, be my helper!"
> You have turned my mourning into dancing;
> You have taken off my sackcloth and clothed me with joy,
> So that my soul may praise you and not be silent.
> O LORD my God, I will give thanks to you forever. (Ps. 30:4–12)

The psalm shifts from an established scene of thanksgiving to one of pious instruction addressing a human audience. Subsequent verses resume address to the Lord, only to embed a recollection in which the speaker laments a personal condition and calls to the Lord for deliverance. The psalm returns to its original frame with the speaker reiterating an experience of deliverance and announcing intentions to extol and give thanks to the Lord, now and ever more. Although it may be characterized as a psalm of thanksgiving, its shifts of focus invite questions about genre and imagined contexts of performance, or what biblical scholars call a text's "Sitz im Leben" (setting in life). Old Testament scholar Walter Brueggemann classifies Psalm 30 with other songs of thanksgiving as "psalms of new orientation," to be distinguished in a functional typology from "psalms of orientation" and "psalms of disorientation" (Psalms 9). Born of a transformative experience, these psalms integrate former states of order and peril.

At issue in Psalm 30 is the potential for response to divine action. Here the human supplicant can be seen to cooperate in the prayed-for deliverance from peril. In other words, the psalm testifies to the power of prayer as a transformative agency, not in a magical sense but as a process of dialogical resolution. In saying, "Will dust acclaim you?" the speaker effectively reminds the Lord that, if destroyed, no speaker can give glory to the Lord's faithfulness. The speaker not only celebrates deliverance from certain death, imagined as being consigned to Sheol, but affirms that the Lord is one who listens. Reframed as a hymn of thanksgiving, this second address also celebrates prayer as a discursive *acting with* more powerful agents.

I stress, then, that prayer is an illocutionary act, one that through the force of utterance contributes to unfolding events perceived as action willed or permitted by divine beings and assented to or challenged by human beings. Beyond a response to divine intervention, prayer itself intervenes. To attribute agency to the divine through acts of invocation is simultaneously to claim a measure of agency for oneself.

One contemporary prayer voices a scene of cooperation in highly self-referential terms: "Somehow, Jesus, I like praying with a cup of coffee in my hands. I guess the warmth of the cup settles me and speaks of the warmth of your love. I hold the cup against my cheek and listen, hushed and still. I blow on the coffee and drink. O Spirit of God, blow across my little life and let me drink in your great life. Amen" (Foster, *Prayers* 44). Working in a Quaker (or Society of Friends) tradition noted for its simplicity, Richard Foster articulates an experience of intimate friendship with Jesus. His text is both a prayer in itself and a didactic model for imagining possibilities for prayer in life's "ordinary" moments. In its embrace of the quotidian, this "coffee prayer" will strike some as lacking in gravitas. Its natural stance quietly shocks our expectation of elaborate gestures and elevated language. The contrast between the formality of the prayers examined above and the familiarity of this prayer invites consideration of their respective scenes: on the one hand, physical and verbal overtures of humility ostentatiously performed, yet fitting the perceived relationship between speaker and addressee; and on the other, physical (praying with cup in hand) and verbal overtures audacious in their simplicity, yet likewise fitting the perceived relationship between speaker and addressee. Each of these prayers employs stylistic resources deemed appropriate to the particular invocation being performed.

The Jesus addressed in Foster's prayer is a breakfast companion; only at the prayer's conclusion does a conversational tone cede to an elevated vocative, "O Spirit of God," to introduce a formal, if playfully figured, apostrophe: "blow across my little life and let me drink in your great life." This appeal reminds us that this prayer, for all its immediacy, is also an invocation calling upon the (Holy) Spirit to be an animating, inspirational force in the speaker's "little life." The seemingly unconventional image of Spirit blowing across the surface of a liquid both to cool and to disturb it is meant to invoke a foundational image from the book of Genesis in the Breath (Hebrew *ruach,* meaning "air" or "wind") of God moving across "the face of the waters" (1:2) at the moment of Creation.

An invocation, I stress, is more than an initiating move to gain the attention of a divine audience for some prayer to follow. Invocations are, instead, a frame for discourse. At the same time, certain words and gestures may be said to perform an invocation as formal markers of address. Such invocational markers (e.g., "O Lord") need not appear at a prayer's formal beginning; they may appear elsewhere, even at a prayer's end, or in multiple places within a prayer, which points to their role in establishing and maintaining a scene of address. These stylized vocatives reinforce understanding that an utterance *is* a prayer and not some other form of discourse. What finally satisfies a conventional expectation of prayer in Foster's text is formal recognition of Jesus as addressee and, even more so, recognition of the Holy Spirit as an abiding presence that must yet be invoked.

For not all discourse addressed to divine audiences *counts* as prayer. Conversation, as between God and Abraham (in Genesis) or between God and Moses (in Exodus), is not prayer. Such dialogue lacks a requisite distance to be overcome. Despite talk of prayer as "conversation with God," prayer is not figured in conversational terms.[1] Formality of address ("Dear Jesus" or "Heavenly Father") marks prayer as substantively different from typical conversation. Indeed, prayer can move only so far in the direction of immediacy before the loss of remoteness robs it of rhetorical power in overcoming estrangement. For prayer, there must first *be* estrangement, born of apprehension of distance: some barrier must be broken or impediment transcended.

In certain conceptions of prayer, the divine is already present to human speakers. In this case, invocation, though figured as summoning the divine, is a form of self-summons—a calling *to mind* as much as a calling *upon*. Although, theologically, the difference between these framings may be great, in performative terms, bringing oneself to attention and invocation are two sides of the same coin. Each is accomplished through symbolic forms that summon speaker and audience into mutual presence. Here an emphasis on prayer as scene and as act is particularly pronounced. As a scene of address, prayer is conceived as a mutual presence already established, but yet to be fully acted upon. As an act of invocation, prayer conjures a scene, brings it into being here and now. The motives of scene and act in prayer are a dialectic of stasis and transformation.

Prayer may thus be understood as a techné for generating or maintaining presence—something difficult in any case, but especially where parties in a communicative exchange are distant from each other. In prayer, human beings have the work all on their side without benefit of concrete response in real time. In this respect, as noted, markers of address distributed across an utterance contribute to establishing and maintaining presence. A single vocative does not always sustain an invocation. In performative terms, prayer repeatedly begins anew. Divine presence must continually be invoked, or repeatedly called to mind:

> We have our treasure in earthen vessels, but thou, O Holy Spirit, when thou livest in a man, thou livest in what is infinitely lower. Thou Spirit of Holiness, thou livest in the midst of impurity and corruption; thou Spirit of Wisdom, thou livest in the midst of folly; thou Spirit of Truth, thou livest in one who is himself deluded. Oh, continue to dwell there, thou who dost not seek a desirable dwelling place, for thou wouldst seek in vain, thou Creator and Redeemer, to make a dwelling for thyself; oh, continue to dwell there, that one day thou mayst finally be pleased by the dwelling which thou didst prepare in my heart, foolish, deceiving, and impure as it is. (Kierkegaard, *Prayers* 106)

One senses that this prayer of Søren Kierkegaard could continue with further appellations of Spirit and further commonplaces of the speaker's unworthiness. A single vocative does not sustain the invocation or semantically encompass its object. Rather, Spirit must be called upon repeatedly in order to realize a pleni-tude the prayer would seek to represent. Not every prayer recapitulates an ini-tial calling, of course, but extended formal invocation is a distinctive attribute of prayer—one that makes for a curious conversation. What matters in such appeals is the appeal itself as a renewing opportunity for reverent address. Con-sider this exemplary passage from "Hymn to Matter" of French Jesuit Pierre Teilhard de Chardin:

> Blessed be you, harsh matter, barren soil, stubborn rock: you who would yield only to violence, you who would force us to work if we would eat.
> Blessed be you, perilous matter, violent sea, untamable passion: you who unless we fetter you will devour us.
> Blessed be you, mighty matter, irresistible march of evolution, reality ever newborn: you who, by constantly shattering our mental categories, force us to go ever further and further in our pursuit of the truth.
> Blessed be you, universal matter, unmeasurable time, boundless ether, triple abyss of stars and atoms and generations: you who by overflow-ing and dissolving our narrow standards of measurement reveal to us the dimensions of God. (75–76)

Teilhard de Chardin's "Hymn" is an evocative fusion of the material and the mystical, befitting its composer's double calling as paleontologist and theolo-gian. A century later, its imagined scene of address still has power to shock. Profoundly Catholic, though hardly orthodox—Teilhard de Chardin's philo-sophical writings were suppressed in his lifetime—this hymn to matter (rather than to Spirit) leads deeper into complexities of prayer as an act of invocation and makes for an intriguing contrast with Kierkegaard's oration to Spirit.

"Hymn to Matter" appears in Teilhard de Chardin's *Hymn of the Universe* as a visionary discourse. It stages a soliloquy in which a single speaker, represent-ing a chorus of humanity, addresses the fullness of Creation as if Creation pos-sessed agency of its own. A tour de force in *copia*, or amplification of an idea, the hymn's use of anaphora in its repeated appeals echoes Burke's description of the scene of address as one progressing toward an ideal of *courtship* in contrast to easy conversation among equals. Indeed, "courtship" may be understood here in both a romantic and a political sense as language employed "for the transcending of social estrangement" (*RM* 208). The hymn's iterative strategy in continually addressing "matter" seems to manifest Burke's notion of "pure persuasion": a rhetorical overture that "involves the saying of something, not for an extra-verbal advantage to be got for the saying, but because of a satisfaction intrinsic to the saying. It summons because it likes the feel of a summons" (*RM* 269). Thus does invocation, conceptually an opening move, resist *closure* to maintain a prayer, to keep it going. To call upon an object of address is, in a sense, the point. This is not to say, however, that invocation lacks practical design. Invocation may manifest the purity of appeal in principle, but it is not without other ends. Only in the most rarefied contexts is prayer simply a matter of keeping company with its object of address. Invocations are acts of address at their most stylized and strategic.

The crucial aspect of the repeated articulation of divine names is that an audience is conceived as not immediately or not fully present. A divine audience is conceived as belonging to another world—potentially addressable, yet remote—elsewhere, in a significant way. Alternatively, human speakers and human audiences are never fully present within a scene of communication. Communicative presence is never long sustained, even under the best of circumstances. By design, prayer's formal structures respond to this challenge to establish and maintain an authentic communicative space against pressures urging its dissolution.

The ideal communicative space to which prayer strives is one that manifests an "I-Thou" relationship, as famously characterized by philosopher Martin Buber (1878–1965). In *I and Thou*, Buber contrasts a dialogic "I-Thou" with an objectivizing "I-It" relationship. In an "I-It" relationship, the other is reduced to a *thing* in the environment of the self, whereas an "I-Thou" relationship is a two-way mode of address that demands the opening of the self to the other. This dialogic model of call and response undergirds an ethic of responsibility to the world at large. In relation to prayer in particular, Buber characterizes God as an "eternal Thou," even if human beings would reduce a relationship with God to one of "I-It." "The eternal Thou can by its nature not become an It; it cannot be understood as a sum of qualities, not even as an infinite sum of qualities raised to a transcendental level" (85). Buber's "eternal Thou" is insistently personal and at the same time entirely abstract, lest assigning attributes other than pure relation and addressability rob God of radical otherness.

According to Buber, the scene of encounter with the eternal Thou intensely humanizes its praying subject: "The I of the primary word I-Thou is a different

I of the primary word I-It. The I of the primary word I-It makes its appearance as individuality and becomes conscious of itself as subject (of experiencing and using). The I of the primary word I-Thou makes its appearance as person and becomes conscious of itself as subjectivity (without a dependent genitive). Individuality makes its appearance by being differentiated from other individualities. A person makes his appearance by entering into relation with other persons" (51). Buber's dialogism is significant for rhetoric, though more for its imagined purity (as a foil to reductive discourse) than for its descriptive plenitude.

Buber's dialogic I-Thou anticipates Mikhail Bakhtin's more robust notions of utterance. In "The Problem of Speech Genres," Bakhtin recognizes that an utterance—the smallest unit of pragmatic discourse—may occur in multiple contexts, from monologic outburst addressed to no one in particular to address that participates in the construction of interpersonal dialogue. For Bakhtin, dialogic discourse is a series of anticipated and responsive turn takings. Stressing that different speech genres differently embody utterance, Bakhtin places genres that realize possibilities for dialogue at a privileged end of a discursive range. In "Reworking the Dostoevsky Book," he explains: "The single adequate end for verbally expressing authentic human life is the open-ended dialogue. Life by its very nature is dialogic. To live means to participate in dialogue: to ask questions, to heed, to respond, to agree, and so forth. In this dialogue a person participates wholly and throughout his life: with his eyes, lips, hands, soul, spirit, and with his whole body and deeds. He invests his entire self in discourse, and the discourse enters into the dialogic fabric of human life, into the world symposium" (293). Bakhtin's dynamic dialogism has obvious resonances with a scene of prayer. All that is required to imbue this dialogue with a distinctly religious cast is to add asymmetry in the form of hierarchical relations between interlocutors. This asymmetry of rank, power, and presence in the scene of address is precisely what prayer in its character as invocation seeks to realize at the level of performance.

Invocation and Apostrophic Address

Having identified crucial features of appeal in the performatives of invocation as opportunities to realize a scene of address in action, let us now turn to features that productively complicate the presumed purity of this act. Surprisingly, prayer does not thrive on purity but on an inherent messiness in bridging through discourse the ontological divide between human and divine. As a rhetorical act, invocation both establishes a scene of mutual presence and addresses some higher power. These are quite differently motivated acts.

This conceptual stance informs any verbal act of address and distinguishes invocation from the merely figural gesture of apostrophe. Despite a surface similarity, differences between invocation and apostrophe are crucial to the rhetoric of prayer. In this respect, we can distinguish between acts of calling that sincerely intend to achieve verbal communion with their objects of address and other, similar vocative acts that have no such intent. Yet this distinction, easily made in principle, is difficult to make in practice across the range of discursive acts. As Buber and Bakhtin recognize, the object of address is ever in danger of being objectified as a discursive prop in a figurative scene of address. The risk of idolatry or blasphemy in calling out to the divine is considerable.

Although the figure of apostrophe has a long, complex history, with considerable disagreements over its meaning and significance, several points can help us usefully compare it with the act of invocation. Literally a "turning away" (Greek *apo* + *strophein*), *apostrophe* marks a discursive scene in which a speaker turns his or her attention from an audience to address some absent person or personified abstraction. The *Rhetorica ad Herennium* (c. 70 BCE) defines *apostrophe* as a figure of diction that "expresses grief or indignation by means of an address to some man or city or place or object" (283).[2] The connection between emotional outburst and appeal to a remote addressee is as complex as it is provocative. Apostrophe, it would appear, arises from a condition, whether genuine or feigned, of being overcome by joy, grief, or anger. One is effectively transported to a place represented by the figure to whom one cries out, a figure that breaks from an established discursive frame with a new scene of address. Significantly, the figure can be as much a device for performing a stance before an audience as a genuine experience of transport.

This is the sense in which Jonathan Culler discusses apostrophe's role in lyric poetry in *The Pursuit of Signs*. Citing John Stuart Mill's aphorism that the lyric is not heard, but overheard, Culler classifies uses of the vocative as "intensifiers" and "images of invested passion" in implicit agreement with the conceptual merger of apostrophe and ecphonesis (137). On the one hand, apostrophe is audience centered, placed in a complex space of address involving hearing and overhearing. One speaks to an audience, then momentarily turns away from it to address another. On the other hand, apostrophe is a phenomenon of a performer's mental state—what Pierre Fontanier refers to in *Figures du discours* as "the spontaneous impulse of a powerfully moved soul" (372, translation mine). Apostrophe thus exemplifies the classic division between poetic and rhetorical, expressive and strategic, modes of discourse. Culler goes beyond these dichotomies to identify in apostrophe the power of language "to will a state of affairs, to attempt to call it into being by asking inanimate objects to bend themselves to your desire" (139).

Suggesting that readers of the lyric not be too quick to dismiss appeals to inanimate objects as merely figurative descriptions, Culler proposes that apostrophe moves toward I-Thou relationships between speaking subjects and addressed objects "to make the objects of the universe potentially responsive forces: forces that can be asked to act or refrain from acting or even to continue behaving as they would usually behave" (139). Given how closely apostrophe resembles a scene of prayer in Culler's description, it comes as no surprise that he refers to apostrophe as "embarrassing: embarrassing to me and to you" (155). Should we go all the way, then, and equate the apostrophe of lyric poetry with the invocation of prayer? We can find no reason not to at the level of form. The vocative structures of prayer resemble those of lyric, down to the exclamatory "O" as sign of urgency and intensity. Moreover, the exclamatory "O" signifies an addressee's remoteness; one must strain to reach this audience. Only in context is prayer distinguishable from apostrophic address.

The distinction between apostrophe and invocation lies in hearing, as opposed to overhearing. Prayer's primary purpose is to be heard, not overheard. In apostrophe, a primary speech situation anticipates address to an absent audience and positions its present (human) audience as overhearers. Even when prayer *is* overheard, it does not position human audiences as overhearers. Prayer's human audiences are conceived as affirmative participants, never purely as auditors. By contrast, one need not assent to a poem to admire it, enter its imaginative world, or even be transported by it. Indeed, the reader of lyric is moved at some level by the experience of transport of an implied speaker to whom the reader serves as overhearing witness. A lyric poem requires both a remote addressee and a human audience to experience this address as an apostrophe.

The relationship between speaker, addressee, and auditor thus differs significantly in prayer and apostrophe. Although prayer manifests sophisticated structures of address, direct and indirect, explicit and implicit, to both divine and human audiences, its scene of address is not within some *other* discursive frame. There is no primary audience whose attention must first be obtained so that it can be experienced as not addressed or even as turned from. Not so for apostrophe. Culler recognizes the rhetorical danger of apostrophe in a paradox "that this figure which seems to establish relations between the self and the other can be read as an act of radical interiorization and solipcism" (146). By substituting an idol of our own making for the one to which we appeal, we reduce our appeal to a matter of artifice.

A final source of embarrassment in apostrophe is that its transcendent effects are all too easily achieved: "Apostrophe must be repressed precisely because this high calling of poetry must not be seen to depend on a trope, an 'O.' This trope proclaims its artificial character rather too obviously, and the craft of poetry would be demeaned if it were allowed that any versifier who wrote 'O table' were approaching the condition of sublime poet" (Culler 152). What applies to poetry here applies to prayer as well. Figures of address can overwhelm their scene, resulting in artfully dialogic soliloquy.

The Phenomenology of Invocation: Levinas, Derrida, and Marion

Faced with the impossibility of adequately addressing the divine, prayer's most astute observers approach scenes of articulate address in fear and trembling, to echo Kierkegaard. Such trepidation arises, in large part, from the prospect of addressing the God of monotheism. Yet it might well be claimed that this God is at some level an effect of recognizing profound ethical implications inherent in performing address. Three continental philosophers, Emmanuel Levinas, Jacques Derrida, and Jean-Luc Marion, have posed significant challenges to the rhetoric of invocation in ways that resonate with Culler's intimations of danger. For Culler, this danger is situated in solipsism afforded by an apostrophic "O." For these philosophers, it lies in the predication that follows from the vocative "O."

Even a brief exposition of the philosophers' respective positions on the possibility of divine address is eye opening with respect to prayer as a site of rhetorical action. At issue is the (im)possibility of adequate language for addressing God. Exploring concerns articulated by Buber, Emmanuel Levinas (1906–95) recognizes the scene of address as fundamentally ethical in the encounter with the other: "The essential is the interpellation, the vocative" (*Totality* 69). Levinas proceeds to identify invocation, recognition of the other *as* other, as the only language in which the other is respected, despite the risk of violence in the address: "The other is maintained and confirmed in his heterogeneity *as soon as one calls upon him*" (69, emphasis in original).

For Levinas, the ethical encounter is one of pure address: "The ethical relation, the face-to-face, also cuts across every relation one could call mystical, where events other than the presentation of the original being come to overwhelm or sublimate the pure sincerity of this presentation, where intoxicating equivocations come to enrich the primordial univocity of expression, where discourse becomes incantation, as prayer becomes rite and liturgy, where the interlocutors find themselves playing a role in a drama that has begun outside of them" (*Totality* 201). He seeks to preserve a scene of encounter before a descent into rhetoric, a discursive scene in which principles of division and strategy substitute for "pure sincerity." Levinas opposes the incantation of poetry to the sincerity, and immediacy, of prose: "Discourse is rupture and commencement, breaking of rhythm which enraptures and transports the interlocutors—prose" (202). To be fully ethical, prayer must free itself from poetry.

Levinas's position on the separation of the ethical and the aesthetic is intriguing, even troubling, for one can readily discern in the aesthetic a source of corruption to the purity of the vocative. A language of praise, for example, in its heightened affective character, reflects back on its performers in ways that a pure language of address, assuming there is such a thing, does not. In a later essay, Jacques Derrida (1930–2004) echoes this concern of Levinas about prayer as a scene of address: "In every prayer there must be an address to the other as other, and I will add, at the risk of shocking you, *God, for example.* In the act of addressing oneself to the other as other one must, of course, pray, that is ask, implore, summon. It does not matter what one is asking for; pure prayer asks only that the other hear the prayer, receive it, be present to it, be the other as such, gift, call and the very cause of prayer" (176, emphasis in original). The prayer Derrida imagines is one of pure possibility, the purest of speech acts, before its actual utterance requires predication that turns the vocative into the constative. Derrida would maintain a crucial distinction between the call as invitation, the call to come, to be present, and the act of naming, which projects the self onto the other, denying its otherness even as it professes to open itself to the other. For Derrida, prayer is pure "O ____"—without the name.

At issue is whether the other is "wholly other" (*le tout autre*), which, for Derrida, the other must be. Hence the distinction between prayer addressed to the radically other and prayer that invokes the *known* other through assertion of some relationship of identity. This identity is the basis of a response beyond the call. The possibility of no response is something Derrida insists upon in recognizing this radically, wholly other. J. Hillis Miller observes that the call to Derrida's wholly other is less a demand placed upon the other than it is a response to the other: "Such a response is to some degree passive or submissive. It obeys a call or command. All we can do is profess faith in the call or pledge allegiance to it. Only such a speech act constitutes a genuine event that breaks the predetermined course of history" (5).

Derrida's critique of a metaphysics of presence allows for the impossibility of calling upon the other. Seeking a way around the impasse created by opposing the disinterest of pure address to the strategic interest of invocation, a rhetoric of invocation assigns a name, or names, to what it addresses, a distinction that echoes Levinas's concerns about ethical and aesthetic discourse.

A third philosophical voice on the rhetoric of invocation is that of Jean-Luc Marion, whose phenomenological account of an encounter with the other in prayer resonates with concerns about an ethics of address on the part of both Levinas and Derrida. For Marion, radical distinctions between petition and praise, pure address and impure invocation, are not insurmountable. To overcome those differences, Marion proposes that divine names are a pragmatic strategy for addressing an other that is beyond signification: "Not only does naming not contradict the invocation of the prayer, but without invocation the prayer would be impossible—what would it mean to praise without praising anyone, to ask without asking from anyone, to offer a sacrifice without offering it to anyone?" (*In Excess* 144). Marion argues for the obligation to continue anyway in petition and especially in praise, even while recognizing the inadequacy of language to properly name the divine: "The approach of prayer always consists of de-nominating—not naming properly, but setting out to intend God [*le viser*] in all impropriety" (144). Marion's essentially pragmatic approach allows for the insufficiency of naming precisely because he accepts a reality beyond, or in excess of, what any name circumscribes. Recognizing this insufficiency is tantamount to recognizing at a fundamental level the unnameability of God, for Marion's reading of prayer occurs entirely in a Christian context.

Christina M. Gschwandtner detects an effort to "protect God in [Marion's] accounts of prayer" from any form of idolatry: Marion's "analysis of prayer [therefore] tends to dissolve into a concern about how the individual can speak rightly about God"; it emphasizes individual experience of prayer over its "communal aspect" (169). And it does so, I hasten to add, in ways that Levinas's and Derrida's accounts do not. Despite their dissimilar characterization of the other in the act of address, both Levinas and Derrida articulate an ethics of inter-personal relation, whereas Marion is concerned, ultimately, with an aesthet-ics of reception. In this respect, Marion illuminates precisely the core concern of Levinas about the conflict between an ethics and an aesthetics of invoca-tion. Moreover, he exposes the Achilles heel of phenomenology in its failure to articulate satisfactorily a connection between the individual and the social. As Gschwandtner observes, "Marion is more interested in what prayer cannot say than in what it can or should say" (178).

Actual prayer, in its rhetorical richness, is always both an apostrophe to the other and an invocation that returns *from* the other, back to the domain of the social. An invocation is also a vocation: an act of address places demands on speaker and audience alike. It is never a pure scene of address, but an impure or improper appeal with designs on its reciprocal agents. To be clear, invocation is ever political: it never transcends the social in its outreach to the other. Its turn to the other is signaled by "O"; its return, by an "Amen" that marks a commit-ment to some vision articulated in the prayer.

That said, as invocation, prayer does not simply conclude by returning to an original frame: its scene is open ended. Articulated as a response to a situ-ation and itself situated in a present moment, an invocation creates a horizon of possibility by its utterance. Advancing toward that horizon, an invocation is a quintessentially commissive speech act. It seeks to bring some hoped-for state of affairs into existence. Whatever form the acts of prayer assume (explicit invocation, petition, confession), the frame of those acts is one in which prayer's speakers commit themselves to the truth and force of their utterance through the performatives of invocation. That is to say, prayer's speakers recognize with trepidation the power of their own discourse to bring a state of affairs into being. Or, again, invocations are dangerous rhetorical acts.

Rhetorical Strategies of Invocation: Naming the Divine

In this final section, we consider how naming the divine may be used to main-tain or challenge the status quo or to pursue a commitment to some vision of the real. This is invocation as specifically vocative, whether salutational or interwoven within a larger utterance. The opening lines from a contemporary anthology of prayers illustrate the range of prayerful vocatives:

O God,

O fathers and ancestors, and all who are of near and far past,

O creator, who dost all human beings create,

God of the generations,

Lord,

O immeasurably tender love! O everlasting Light!

Dear Jesus,

O our Mother the earth,

O God, creator of our land, our trees, the animals, and humans,

Blessed sister, holy mother, spirit of the fountain, spirit of the garden,

Great Spirit, whose dry lands thirst,

My Lord God,

O Most human Lord and generous giver, sovereign of all things green
    and of the grain, Lord of the earthly paradise,

O Blessed One, eternal Source and Lord of Creation, sustainer of all worlds,

My Sun! My Morning Star!

Lord of incense,

O You four powers of the Universe, you wingeds of the air, and all
    peoples who move through the universe, (Ford-Grabowsky passim)

Some of these vocatives consist only of a name or a title; others embed a salutation in a descriptive claim of attributes. Many employ prototypical titles familiar in Judeo-Christian tradition ("God," "Lord," "Jesus," "Father," "Creator"). Still others exemplify different traditions or push traditional boundaries (Mother," "Great Spirit," "Lord of incense"). Such a list indicates that explicit markers of address are never neutral acts of naming. Each places claims on both speaking and listening agents in a scene of address.

The range of titles by which particular divine beings may be addressed varies across traditions, of course. Some allow for a rich profusion of proper names and metaphorical constructions. Other traditions, respectful of the power inherent in divine names, tread lightly around their use or even proscribe certain names altogether. Indeed, avoidance of a holy name—lest it be used in vain—can lead to substitutes and circumlocutions, such as "Adonai" and "Lord, Master of the Universe" in place of "Yahweh."

Despite customary limitations on forms of divine address, what stands out is that the prayer breaks through walls of conformity to speak anew to situations or to breathe new life into old forms. A traditional prayer may be articulated with fresh insight into its personal or communal relevance, as when references to God as "Father" or "Mother" are mined for emergent meanings. At other times, prayer may depart from accepted discourse to speak in a more prophetic voice. Attention to prayer's character as invocation allows us to hear its potential for transformational agency.

In a sense, all prayer is prophetic to the extent that it calls upon a future situation in the process of becoming. So long as prayer is not a rote act of tradition, its character as prophetic discourse can be pronounced. By articulating an expressly alternative stance, prayer challenges the status quo, creatively engages tradition, and redefines the boundaries of prayerful discourse. Every tradition is sensitive to its stylistic resources, and especially to their violation. For example, those who insist on carrying the archaic "thee" and "thou" into the present age profess a piety that challenges those who use the now conventional "you." Likewise, the use of gender-neutral language to refer to God in many Christian churches draws battle lines about the nature of the divine and of tradition. Traditional practitioners of prayer know to stand guard against accidental (or intentional) lapses in norms of address, for it is in invocational modes that a politics of religious identity is most clearly played out.

The strategic character of invocation can be seen in contemporary efforts to "rename" God in ways that admit of different conceptions of the divine. These efforts often reflect feminist or environmentalist sensibilities that open deep-seated conceptions of the divine to new possibilities. Notably, the contemporary Goddess movement has from its beginning contrasted itself with the dominant Western religious faith traditions of Judaism, Christianity, and Islam. In doing so, this movement challenges paradigms of divine address as knowingly as the psalms advance theological and political ends through cultic hymns. According to Starhawk (Miriam Simos), a leader in this movement, "to invoke the Goddess is to awaken the Goddess within, to become, for a time, that aspect we invoke" (111). This equation of speaker and addressee explicitly connects invocation and identity. In "thealogical" terms, Starhawk articulates a vision of divine immanence *in* the world rather than divine transcendence *beyond* the world. In her vision, the figurative possibilities of invocation play a vital role.

A prayer from a related emerging tradition offers a window onto invocation's rhetorical power:

Living Spirits of Earth
Mother and Father of us all
You who hold us in Your breath
You who bathe us in Your waters
You who feed us with Your fruits
Guardian of where we are going, of who we are becoming
Cradle of our days and coffin of our nights
You who carry us folded in Your arms
Sailing silently among the stars
Hear our prayers. (*Life Prayers* 6)

A succinct expression of nature-oriented religion, this prayer invokes the Earth as "Mother and Father of us all." Even more than other prayers featured in this chapter, this prayer is *all* invocation—a series of predications of "You" as a sustaining body. Appropriate to its initiating function, the prayer adopts a preparatory stance to further discourse by inviting its divine addressees and human speakers to attend (hear) what prayers may follow. In acknowledging our deep connection to and dependence on a nurturing Earth, however, it is itself a complete prayer. The "creedal" claims of this address articulate a consequential pledge to honor and protect the Earth as the Earth protects its inhabitants. To respond to the Earth through this invocation is to take responsibility for it by bringing one's action's into conformity with one's words. In this rhetorical exchange, the act of invocation (calling upon) thus involves a reciprocal acceptance of vocation (being called).

The necessary emphasis in invocation, then, is on prayer as rhetorical *action* rather than as belief or, in speech-act-theoretic terms, on performative rather than constative utterance. Invocation is thus conceived as a strategy for realizing the real through imaginative commitment to some existing or emerging order. The shift in emphasis from a motive of scene to one of act allows for a necessary, if still incomplete, account of prayer as a site of rhetorical action. A focus on prayer as invocation (over other modes) emphasizes the interactive, cooperative relationship between human and divine agents. At the same time, prayer respects the limits of human agency in the face of more powerful divine beings. The relationship of human to divine is ultimately one of hierarchy and dependence. Where invocation demands, "Come!" a spirit of reverence remembers, "Please."

4

THE DANCE OF ATTITUDE:
PRAYER AS THE PERFORMANCE OF REVERENCE

I propose to call hope an attitude. By this I mean that it is a set or disposition
of the whole person, a stance or posture which one takes up toward experience
or sectors of experience, and from which one relates to such experience.

—John Macquarrie, *Christian Hope*

Always beneath the dance of words there will be the dance of bodies.

—Kenneth Burke, *The Rhetoric of Religion*

I am told that, during the height of "the troubles" in Northern Ireland, a cartoon ran in a British newspaper whose satiric target was the Reverend Ian
Paisley, member of Parliament and leader of the Democratic Unionist Party, a
fiercely Protestant faction. The cartoon depicted Paisley alone, cassocked and
kneeling atop a windswept hill in Ulster as storm clouds roil menacingly above.
An angry fist held high, the Reverend Paisley bellows, "Now, You listen to Me,
God!" In this picture and voice is a perfect image of irreverence: Paisley fails,
spectacularly, in knowing where he is.

An ideal counterpart to this scene appears in the incident of the "burning
bush" in the Old Testament book of Exodus: "When the Lord saw that [Moses]
had turned aside to see, God called to him out of the bush, 'Moses, Moses!' And
[Moses answered,] 'Here I am.' Then he said, 'Come no closer! Remove the sandals from your feet, for the place on which you are standing is holy ground.' He
said further, 'I am the God of your father, the God of Abraham, the God of Isaac,
and the God of Jacob.' And Moses hid his face, for he was afraid to look at God"
(3:4–6). Among the insights encapsulated in this pivotal moment in the history of
Judaism is this: to encounter the divine, one must know where one stands, for the
place one meets the divine is always holy ground—a space set apart. Moses demonstrates he is the appropriate one to receive this revelation and mission because
he knows where he stands. When the Lord reveals himself, Moses responds

accordingly, removing his sandals as commanded and shielding his face. The first act is a gesture of humility. The second is a measure of awe—fear's complement. Significantly, the response by Moses to divine revelation is primarily physical. In responding to the divine, the body speaks as tellingly as words.

Between the physical and verbal poles of upraised fist and angry demand at one pole and bared feet and responsive "Here I am!" at the other lie all possible responses to an encounter with the divine. The Moses of Exodus and the Paisley of political lampoon epitomize piety and impiety, respectively, in their apprehension of this encounter. One succeeds and the other fails in manifesting "*a sense of what properly goes with what*" that Kenneth Burke identifies as the essence of piety (*PC* 74, emphasis in original). Above all, it is the manner of performance that is critical here.

The rhetoric of prayer hinges on distinctions manifested in the revelation of attitude. That Moses embodies a proper attitude of receptivity in his encounter with the Lord is evident enough. Yet we can do more than declare for Moses against a convenient foil by recognizing that the similarities in these scenes matter as much as their differences. In both, word and gesture reveal an internal disposition, a habit of mind, and an orientation toward the situations in which speakers find themselves and the audiences before whom they speak. Each performs an *attitude* as a stylized response to this situation. Only Moses responds fittingly to his actual situation.

To extrapolate from these instances, we might regard prayer not as a particular activity but as the character of an action. Beyond explicit forms of verbal appeal to the divine, other activities, indeed all of life, can be a prayer insofar as their performance is marked by a character of mindfulness, joy, and receptivity. Thus baking bread, patiently enduring difficulty, or appreciating nature's bounty can be a prayer.[1] The virtues manifested in these activities are those we associate with prayer as a fusion of act and attitude.

This chapter concerns itself with the relationship between prayer as a formal act and as a proper attitude or, more precisely, with the rhetorical character of prayer as the manifestation of attitude *through* act. I argue that prayer is the performance of attitude, specifically an attitude of reverence, the attitude most characteristic of prayer in its many forms and concerns. Here I define *reverence* as "a discerning and gracious acceptance of one's subordinate, contingent place within an ordered and hierarchical cosmos."

I thus offer two related claims: prayer is a manifestation of attitude; and "reverence" is a fitting label for this attitude. Virtually all accounts of prayer identify

THE DANCE OF ATTITUDE

reverence as its quintessential attitude. Ole Hallesby characterizes prayer as "a definite attitude of our hearts toward God, an attitude which He in heaven immediately recognizes as prayer" (18). This claim echoes a Bahai belief that "prayer need not be in words, but rather in thought and attitude" (Bahá'u'lláh qtd. in Esslemont 94). The attitude of reverence may be understood as both internal disposition and external manner of performance. Reverence invests acts with piety to make them prayerful. Of course, other terms for prayer's quintessential attitude suggest themselves, including *awe*, *desire*, and *gratitude*. These affective states all figure in reverence, whose scope extends beyond religion per se to spiritualized dimensions of the secular. Moreover, reverence exceeds affect in being rhetorical performance. Not simply a feeling or state, reverence must be performed before particular audiences.

A chapter on *attitude* forms a "trinity" with preceding chapters on *scene* and *act*. Chapter 2 drew upon Burkean principles of dramatism to articulate a model of prayer as a scene of address, one that imaginatively expands the sphere of human social relations to include significant otherworldly audiences. The emphasis here is on the shared linguistic ground that makes communication possible between human and divine agents. Chapter 3 likewise drew upon dramatism and insights from speech-act theory to approach prayer as verbal action. Transposing the terms of a scene-act relation to an act-scene one shifts emphasis to formal utterance, specifically to invocation as prayer's central performative. In its focus on attitude, this chapter, too, is grounded in Burke's dramatism, though with a twist.

Attitude is a sixth motive Burke retrospectively added to his original five in recognition that the pentad would be better as a hexad. "I have sometimes added the term 'attitude' to the above list of five major terms," says Burke in an addendum to the 1969 edition of the *Grammar of Motives*, explaining that "'attitude' would designate the manner (*quo modo*)" by which an act is performed (443). "Attitude" is distinguishable from "agency," the means by which an act is performed, though manner and means may be conflated in expressions of *how* an act is performed, such as "with a hammer" or "confidently" (443). That said, I propose that "attitude" supplies the "something more" required to account for prayer.

Significantly, prayer itself links attitude to other motives. The connections between attitude and prayer explored in this chapter offer a compelling rationale for the pentad's expansion. Burke's modification hearkens back to his prior accounts of attitude, notably in *Attitudes Toward History*, where he identifies attitudes as "incipient acts" (348). Here one can see a nascent formulation of the concept of relations ("ratios"), later developed in the *Grammar of Motives*. Exploring relations formed by *attitude* and other motives, especially *act*, sheds light on prayer as a rhetoric.

The chapter begins by reading Burke's characterization of "secular prayer" as a manifestation of attitude. It then examines praise as a site for the performance of reverence, delineating the challenge of performing praise as discourse that negotiates a proper balance between authenticity and artistry, inspiration and ego. Next, it moves beyond praise to consider fundamental matters of dependence, hierarchy, and transcendence as these bear on reverence, with an extended reading of a single speech event in the Kwakiutl culture of the Pacific Northwest. I close the chapter by arguing that reverence is best understood as the perfection of the rhetorical principle itself—the apotheosis of appeal.

Praying with Attitude: A Matter of Coaching and Dancing

At the heart of prayer is the relationship between devotional acts and their dispositions. As important as semantic content and purpose are, what really matters is *how* prayer is performed. It must be undertaken in the proper spirit and executed with care. Indeed, prayer's perceived difficulty, even impossibility absent divine assistance in the view of some, speaks to prayer's affective complexity as performance. Saint Paul famously observes that "we do not know how to pray as we ought, but the very Spirit intercedes with sighs too deep for words. And God, who searches the heart, knows what is the mind of the Spirit, because the Spirit intercedes for the saints according to the will of God" (Rom. 8:26–27). Thus the challenge of prayer is not to find the proper words but to perform those words with a proper spirit.[2]

How prayer is performed characterizes the dramatic relationships between prayer's speakers and its audiences. As we have seen in previous chapters, prayer is discourse that seeks to characterize those relationships by spelling out their situation through symbolic performance. Although we cannot determine definitively the character of any act, which is always a site of negotiation between audience and performer, we can say that each act has its corresponding attitude. Indeed, an act cannot help but communicate an attitude, one given significance by its symbolic markers. Attitudes are socially agreed upon characterizations of what particular acts do and what they communicate. In this respect, candor is a performance of attitude, as is patience or a sense of entitlement. Although the soul may be stirred to true prayer by the activity of praying, when an attentive mind or desiring heart is absent in the performance of prayer, the act becomes mere lip service—going through the motions. In a classic statement on prayer from a Reformed church perspective, theologian Karl Barth observes: "Prayer must be an act of affection; it is more than a question of using the lips, for God asks the allegiance of our hearts. If the heart is not in it, if it is only a form which is carried out more or less correctly, what is it then? Nothing! All prayers offered solely by the lips are not only superfluous, but they are also displeasing to God; and they are not only useless, they are offensive to God" (39).

As much as one can appreciate Barth's insight into the affective dimension of prayer, his privileging of "heart" over "lips" is a radical cleavage of inner disposition and outer form. It is almost as if Barth would protect the pure heart from any impurity imparted by bodily performance. No doubt he would claim he was simply warning against the dangers of hypocrisy and the spirit-deadening effects of routine. Yet, echoing John Calvin, Barth's assertion that "we must think and speak in a *comprehensible* tongue, in a language that has meaning for us," unmistakably gives primacy to intention over form, spirit over letter (39–40, emphasis added).[3] Here at least, Barth does not entertain even the possibility that form itself may take the lead through its instructive effect on the heart.

Perhaps I read too much into his words, seeing them as an expression of a mind-body dualism that is a hallmark of modernism. Nonetheless, I find Barth's call to bring praying heart and praying lips into alignment, with its emphasis on one-way movement from attitude to act, to be only half right. I argue for a *two-way* circulation between heart and lips, attitude and act. In my two-way model, acts invariably communicate, even betray, an attitude, but the reverse is equally true. Acts *form* attitudes. The complementary relations of acts and attitudes are evident in prayer as a domain where habit and character are fused. As a technology of spiritual transformation, prayer seeks to become what it performs, recognizing that only through performance is transformation achievable. It is therefore no surprise that Kenneth Burke looks to prayer for some "perspective by incongruity" in his analysis of prevalent attitudes of "acceptance and rejection" (*ATH* 308–9, 1). In *Attitudes Toward History,* Burke analyzes "secular prayer"—verbal ministrations in the sociopolitical realm—as analogue to religious prayer (321). Secular prayer functions to confront the powers that be on positive terms. Burke employs the oxymoron "secular prayer" to discover strategies of "word magic" hidden in plain sight and operating within technocratic, rationalist discourse (321). In *A Rhetoric of Motives,* Burke claims the discursive operations of prayer do not dissipate in a secular age simply because prayers are no longer directed to deities. Rather, these operations take on a modern cast that involves a shift in vocabulary, not function.

Burke's "secular prayer" is significant for understanding both attitude and prayer in rhetorical terms. Chief among his claims is that "the man who does not 'pray' cannot build his character" (*ATH* 322). As a secular expression of prayer's rhetorical character, this assertion traces the arc from act to attitude that is arguably prayer's primary aim. To pray is to build one's character by inculcating habits of mind.

And of body. For Burke, prayer's manifestation of attitude is not strictly verbal or spiritual. Attitudes are corporeal as well. Burke recognizes the fundamentally multimodal character of prayer in defining "secular prayer" as "the *coaching of an attitude by the use of mimetic and verbal language*" (*ATH* 322; emphasis in original). Burke's juxtaposition of "mimetic and verbal language" emphasizes the body as a site of rhetorical performance.[4] In a key statement of prayer's centrality to rhetoric, Burke maintains: "Secular prayer would not, by our notion, be confined to words. Any mimetic act is prayer. Even 'psychogenic illness' may be a prayer, since it is the 'substantiation of an attitude' in a bodily act. All mimetic procedures, in the dance, the plastic or graphic arts, music, and verbalization are aspects of 'prayer'" (321–22). Here "mimetic procedures" refers to all symbolic representations of interior states. Mimesis, for Burke, is a psychosomatic art rooted in correspondence between the physical and the verbal.

Burke imagines this mimetic correspondence to be most perfectly expressed in the language of dance. In "The Philosophy of Literary Form," Burke identifies any symbolic act as "the *dancing of an attitude*" (*PLF* 9; emphasis in original). As with the language of coaching, the choice of dance for the mimetic realization of attitude underscores its physical dimension. The "coaching" and the "dancing of an attitude" are reciprocal aspects of mimetic performance. We think of coaching in interpersonal terms, some combination of moral guidance and technical instruction by someone to someone. Burke productively complicates this social scene by imagining coaching as something that we can perform upon ourselves. Coaching is intimately bound with performance. We coach (or coax) ourselves to attitude through verbal and other means. We reassure ourselves that things will be all right or steel ourselves to adversity through acts of affirmation. We pray our way to wholeness. This affirmative dimension of prayer is strikingly evident in the divine revelations or "shewings" of fourteenth-century English mystic Julian of Norwich, especially in her revelation "All shall be well, and all shall be well, and all manner of things shall be well" (qtd. in Dutton 55). The performance of any activity is itself an act of coaching in its constructive reinforcement of character—a form of spiritual, but also physical, conditioning.

Thus does Burke identify "secular" prayer to be as discursive as it is bodily. Indeed, Burke effectively grounds spirituality in materiality to the extent that performance is impossible without some instrument. The primary instrument of prayer is the body in both constitutive ("coaching") and expressive ("dancing") senses. Burke's reciprocal formulations of prayer underscore the degree to which prayer *builds* character as much as reveals it.

Burke's equations involving prayer, performance, and character defamiliarize something long recognized in religious contexts: the body, too, prays. In emphasizing the body as a site of mimetic performance, Burke agrees with those who argue for or—in the case of spiritual adepts—act out the character-building, character-revealing aspects of prayer. In the body language of prayer, gesture and posture signify, precisely in their attitudinal character. For how else is prayer possible absent physical comportment? Extending arms or clasping hands; standing, kneeling, or lying prostrate; moving or reposing; facing a compass point; fixing eyes steadily or closing them; lifting head or bowing it—all these gestures, postures, or movements are elements of prayer's corporeal grammar. Reducing prayer to a scene of verbal communication only, or to a mental state, obscures the fully psychosomatic character of all human performance. Yet prayer, in practice, has never entirely forgotten the bodily basis of spiritual communication. In recent years, this embodied character of prayer has been more fully articulated across spiritual traditions.[5] As rhetoric and other disciplines rediscover the body, they likewise rediscover prayer. My reading seeks to restore appreciation for prayer as a rhetorical art in light of this corporeal turn.[6]

That the body mimetically communicates understanding of the divine-human relationship is widely recognized. Thus standing, arms raised, fingers pointed upward is a gesture recognizing the divine in transcendent terms, whereas bowing or lying prostrate is a gesture of humility. The signature gesture of Islam (Arabic for "submission") is the prostrate body oriented toward Mecca. Outer gesture gives expression to the inner attitude it would mimetically induce. Similar correspondences might be traced in the ecstatic whirl of the dervishes of Sufism or the lotus position of Buddhism, where posture is the performance of spiritual insights. The physical sense of attitude as *position* and a corresponding moral sense as *disposition*, a condition of readied response to a stimulus together underscore the etymological descent of "attitude" from aptitude (Latin *aptitudo*, fitness). A sense of fitness, of being in proper shape, to confront certain situation cycles back to notions of coaching.

Among the more notable accounts to fuse scenes of worship with psychosomatic conditioning is the devotional primer "The Nine Ways of Prayer of Saint Dominic" (Modi orandi Sancti Dominici). This modest work (c. 1260–88) celebrates the life of Dominic (1170–1221) and offers itself as a practical rhetoric of prayer (an *ars orandi*) focused on the integrative relations of body and soul. Introducing Dominic's "ways," the text's anonymous author recounts: "What we must say something about here is the way of praying in which the soul uses the members of the body in order to rise more devotedly to God, so that the soul as it causes the body to move, is in turn moved by the body, until sometimes it comes to be in ecstasy like Paul, sometimes in agony like our Saviour, and sometimes in rapture like the prophet David. The blessed Dominic used often to pray like this" (94). The avowed purpose of the text is to verbally describe and pictorially illustrate Dominic at prayer in order to demonstrate the spiritual graces that flow from prayer's various modes, most of which are rooted in a specific posture, such as bowing, kneeling, uplifting one's arms or outstretching them (in imitation of Christ's crucifixion).

In each of these instances, particular dispositions of the body provoke their corresponding affective states, as in this "second" way of prayer: "St. Dominic also often used to pray by throwing himself down on the ground, flat on his face, and then his heart would be pricked by compunction, and he would blush at himself and say, sometimes loudly enough for it actually be to heard, the words from the Gospel, 'Lord, have mercy on me, a sinner'" (Anonymous 96). Here one discovers a perfect instance of the mimetic effects of physical attitudes on their spiritual counterparts. Contrite *action* reinforces contrite words and leads to a contrite *heart*. In its depiction of devotional postures, the text thus serves as a performative grammar for prayer.

Indeed, the history of any spiritual tradition might be told through its devotional gestures. The iconic *orans* (Latin for "praying") posture of arms extended, palms upward became a defining attitude and the dominant visual expression of early Christian prayer, though its use extends much further back in Judaism and other Near Eastern religions. The gesture reads as a statement of openness and confidence in the presence of God. It does so in marked contrast to a servile posture of a slave before a master or a subject before a sovereign: lying prostrate or kneeling, hands clasped together and eyes cast downward. Yet over time, particularly in the Western Catholic Church, the orans posture became the strict province of the priestly celebrant at Mass, whose uplifted hands indicated his mediating role on behalf of the assembly. By contrast, the appropriate posture for the laity in prayer gravitated toward servile gestures.

In recent decades, the orans posture has enjoyed a resurgence in Protestant Pentecostal and Catholic Charismatic circles. Its return is not without controversy. Any gesture signaling a return to the traditions of the early Church is fraught with theological significance. To whom does this gesture belong? What is the appropriate attitude to manifest in public liturgy? Although, from a distance, disputes over appropriate gestures might seem inconsequential, the history of prayer offers ample evidence that such stylistic variations indeed both manifest and magnify profound differences in attitude. They constitute distinct framings of the social situations in which devotional acts are performed.

To see how attention to prayer as attitude contributes to a broader understanding of prayer as a site of rhetorical action, one further reference to Burke's theorizing about attitude proves valuable. In *A Grammar of Motives*, Burke characterizes attitude as "incipient act" (20), a formulation that weaves these terms into a productively tense relationship: we cannot always say at what point an attitude leads to or already begins an act. When an act properly begins and to what extent it flows ineluctably from an antecedent posture or disposition were of sufficient concern to Burke that he wrestled with alternative placements for attitude within the pentad. On the same page where Burke identifies attitude as "*preparation* for an act" or "incipient act," he assigns attitude to another motive, noting that "in its character as a state of *mind* that may or may not lead to an act, [attitude] is quite clearly to be classed under the head of *agent*" (20, emphasis in original).[7] The conundrum of where to place attitude resonates with the qualitative character of prayer straddling a fulcrum that balances "'actus' and 'status'" (20). Prayer is both an act and a state, a matter of both doing and being. In a given context, either *agent* or *act* may be emphasized. Indeed, I do not believe it pushes the metaphor too far to suggest that attitude's "dance" is a two-step, a shift in footing between *character* (as ethical formation) and *action* (as ethical conduct).

Later, in *A Rhetoric of Motives*, Burke writes of a "persuasion 'to attitude' rather than to out-and-out-action" to distinguish the appeal of rhetoric from the force of coercion (50). In struggling to equate attitude now with character, now with act, Burke is clearly troubled by the descriptive inadequacy of the agent-act relation, given the centrality of this relation to the dramatistic scheme as a whole. His identification of *attitude* as a sixth motive mediating somehow between *agent* and *act* seeks to rescue human action from a radical determinism that, Burke continually fears, would reduce action to mere motion. Alternatively, it may be argued that attitude renames agent to highlight the ethical (character-based) dimension of acts as extensions of agents.[8]

In either case, attitude serves as a principle of indeterminacy at once linking and separating motives. Whether Burke's pentad requires a sixth motive or whether attitude is implicit in his original scheme is something we cannot know. It suffices to endorse Burke's realization that some "grammatical" principle of attitude, disposition, or orientation is necessary to account for prayer (and rhetoric as a whole) as a site of ethical encounter between agents. Granting this necessity, we can move to consider strategically appropriate names to assign particular manifestations of attitude. In doing so, we enter the domain of piety, another of prayer's dimensions.

In *Attitudes Toward History*, Burke identifies two fundamental attitudes: "frames of acceptance" and "frames of rejection" (5). *Frames of acceptance* refer to the "more or less organized system of meanings by which a thinking man gauges the historical situation and adopts a role within it," whereas *frames of rejection* identify with "some reigning symbol of authority," an identification that involves a "*shift in allegiance*" from one symbol to another (5; emphasis in original). These frames, or orientations, are an early formulation of concerns Burke revisits in *Permanence and Change*, where he replaces "acceptance" with "piety," variously characterized as a "system builder, a desire to round things out, to fit experiences together into a unified whole," "a schema of orientation," and, with a nod to George Santayana, a "yearning to conform to the 'sources of one's being'" (74, 69). More informally, Burke defines piety as "*a sense of what properly goes with what*" (74, emphasis in original).[9] By contrast, he sees a frame of rejection as one of impiety. Opposing prayer to the impious attitudes of skepticism and cynicism, Burke naturally equates it with a pious attitude in its manifestation as trust, steadfastness, and joy.[10]

Dana Anderson sees in Burke's notions of attitude, piety, and orientation a striking affinity with the concept of "habitus" advanced by sociologist Pierre Bourdieu. According to Anderson, disposition occupies much the same place in Bourdieu's theory of habituated action that attitude does in Burke's dramatistic account. Whereas Burke centers his cluster of terms in "act," Bourdieu structures his in "practice." Bourdieu understands the motive of attitude, identified by Burke as "incipient act," to be "a kind of bodily incipience," a physiological propensity toward action, or an "instilled disposition"—a product or expression of practice (Anderson 270, 257). In simplest terms, attitudes are socially conditioned and embodied, not fleeting responses, but cultivated practices.

This notion of prayer as socially constructed, symbolically expressed, and affectively embodied practice is a critical rounding out of prayer's character as scene or act. Prayer's affective dimension can be described as "habits of the heart," a synecdoche imagined in opposition to "habits of the mind." The purpose of prayer, as the coaching of an attitude, is to cultivate appropriate habits of devotion. Entire vocabularies may be employed to catalog prayer's devotional impulses (desire, awe, fear); these impulses, transformed into habitual practice (authenticity, receptivity, humility), serve as an attitudinal base for the performance of prayer. This development involves a more or less conscious effort to transform situations into strategies, as well as to recognize situations through strategies. Here prayer functions as a critical hermeneutic for reading situations (a point developed more fully in chapter 1).

Mindful of the distinction between momentary impulses and habituated sensibilities, I nominate "reverence" to identify the pious, habitual attitudes of prayer. Through prayer's character-forming resources, an emotional response to situations and stimuli becomes a trained capacity. Depending on its application, prayer can prove a capacitating or incapacitating strategy. The term *reverence* is not offered as a grand summation of all possible terms that might name prayer's basic attitudes. Specifically, reverence is not equivalent to love or desire, as central as these are to a theology of prayer. The choice of "reverence" opens up dimensions of prayer in social and economic terms that by some measure dilute prayer's purity as an affective expression of love or desire. Reverence, I will argue, is as much a behavior as it is a feeling. It places prayer within a virtuous cycle of responsive action.

In chapter 3, I claimed invocation as the core speech act of prayer: absent the bridging of an ontological divide between human speakers and divine audiences through a call to the other *as* other, there can be no prayer. Here I argue that it is through reverence that prayer negotiates this profound divide. Invocation of the divine entails a reciprocal calling, or vocation, for prayer's human speakers to be present to situations. Invocations summon the transformative power of utterance to enact commitments and to shape character. Likewise, the vocation, as answered call, implies some orientation leading to action; it is an attitude in the Burkean sense of an incipient act. This reciprocity between calling upon and being called is what Burke points to in observing that "secular prayer" is both a coaching to and a dancing of attitude.

Because not all prayer will be seen to fall easily under the heading of "reverence," I must clarify how I employ this term. As previously stated, by *reverence* I mean "a discerning and gracious acceptance of one's subordinate, contingent place within an ordered and hierarchical cosmos." Although an attitude of reverence recognizes some moral and material force other than and greater than oneself to serve as a principle of orientation, it need not be *the* principle of orientation. The objects of reverence may be multiple and arranged into various hierarchies and even oppositions. These objects exercise a claim on those who speak from a position of reverence. These claims are not incidental or casual; they are experienced as fundamental to one's individual or collective being. Finally, reverence attributes character to the object of reverence and requires a corresponding affect in the one who performs reverence.

To be clear, reverence is a manner by which a particular audience—not limited to God or the gods—is addressed insofar as that audience is acknowledged as a principle of orientation. The scope of reverence encompasses entities and abstractions (nations, virtues, the Earth) other than deities where these serve as principles of orientation fundamental to one's being. A principle of orientation cannot be reduced to the status of someone or something worthy of esteem; to do so is to set the compass for reverence far too wide. An object of reverence is not merely honored but also, crucially, addressed. The crux of reverence is that this attitude must be performed before an audience conceived as a principle of orientation. For Walter Brueggemann, *orientation* is a key term for the rhetoric of prayer, in particular, prayer as expressed in the Old Testament book of Psalms. In his landmark *The Psalms and the Life of Faith*, Brueggemann takes a functional approach to the psalms in their thematic variations and commonalities through a template that charts "the *movement of orientation, disorientation, and reorientation*" (24, emphasis in original). These orientational stances relate to the primary audience of the Lord addressed in the psalms.

To pray is to go from apprehension of a prayerful situation through an attitude of reverence to an act of address before an appropriate audience. That said, must reverence always occur in the form of an invocation to a divine audience? I submit that reverence may assume forms that challenge a strictly discursive frame, manifested neither in address to a deity nor in any audience at all. A reverence for the Earth, for example, may take form as a conscientious habit of recycling or more profound environmental commitments. Indeed, not to act on a claim of reverence for the Earth or the environment is to pay mere lip service to reverence. A reverence for health may likewise be manifest in "religious" devotion to proper diet and exercise. Given that such devotions guide practice and shape character in ways that are experienced as a call to responsible action, they may be considered legitimate manifestations of reverence or, at least, to approach reverence, conceived in full as a religious practice.

We might, therefore, consider further what forms of intentional and affective response manifesting a reverential attitude can be identified as prayer. Is prayer, finally, a form of address to specific beings apprehended as divine? Or is it a *manner* that infuses various modes of performance with an ethical dimension? Can recycling be prayer? I defer a response to this last question to the conclusion of my study. Here I underscore that Burke's theorizing of the relationship between acts, agents, and attitudes suggests false dichotomies in choosing form over manner, or vice versa, to locate prayer's vital center. It is more productive, I contend, to understand prayer as the overlap of multiple concerns, multiple motives that find their fullest manifestation in reverent address to divine beings.

If anything becomes clearer in this approach, it is that prayer's rhetorical power arises from complex transactions that attitudes negotiate among other motives. I argue that what allows prayer to be recognized across a diverse range of manifestations—what accounts for its dynamic character in addressing multiple audiences across a range of modalities and in various contexts without losing sight of itself as symbolic and embodied performance—is a conceptual core of reverence identifiable in each of its manifestations. I further argue that what gets worked on and worked *out* in prayer are ethical relations between speaker and audience, understood in abstract terms as attitude's relation to form. This is the task assigned to prayer: to discover appropriate forms for the performance of reverence, conceived as an ethical practice of addressing others. In pursuit of this line of inquiry and by way of lending additional texture to this account, let us examine reverence in action, in its character as articulate speech. In other words, let us turn to the language of praise.

Praying with Attitude: The Rhetoric of Praise

According to Richard J. Foster, "adoration is the spontaneous yearning of the heart to worship, honor, magnify, and bless God"; as "selfless devotion," it seeks "nothing but to cherish" God and to see God exalted (*Finding* 81). Adoration thus sets a high aspirational bar for the rhetoric of praise, which may be understood as

the perfection of an impulse to address the divine, disinterestedly and authentically, much as the speaker in Gerard Manley Hopkins's "Pied Beauty":

> Glory be to God for dappled things—
>> For skies of couple-colour as a brinded cow;
>>> For rose-moles all in stipple upon trout that swim . . .
> .   .   .   .
>> Whatever is fickle, freckled (who knows how?)
>>> With swift, slow; sweet, sour; adazzle, dim;
> He fathers-forth whose beauty is past change:
>>>> Praise him.
>>>>>>> (69, 70)

Much admired and frequently anthologized, this late Victorian (1877) poem
is emblematic, for many, of a stance of reverent address in its compelling fusion
of aesthetic and religious sensibility. Rhetorically, it is at once an exhortation to
praise and an act of praise in its own right. It may also be read as a primer on
praise to an age that has forgotten both how to praise and why. "Pied Beauty"
exemplifies what we know about reverence as articulate speech. Who can doubt
the impulse to praise that motivates this poem? Yet, by virtue of its linguistic
and theological subtleties, Hopkins's poem also illustrates the challenges posed
by praise as a formal act.

Two features of praise stand out in "Pied Beauty." First, praise is specific
in identifying attributes worthy of praise in the *object* of praise. Second, and
equally significant, praise is a mode of artistic performance. Thus "Pied Beauty"
is specific in its reasons for glorifying God. Through illustration, accumulation,
and counterpoint, the poem argues that God justly merits praise on account
of the variegated wonders to be met in Creation and the surpassing constancy
of its Creator (at one level, "Pied Beauty" is a theology of beauty).[11] Thus also
the poem is an epideictic occasion—a rhetoric of display. As such, it seeks to
be admired. By design, "Pied Beauty" prompts something more than simple
assent. In its character as art, it resonates with a musical quality. Technically a
curtal (or shortened) sonnet of ten and one-half lines, "Pied Beauty" is idiosyncratic in its lyricism and exemplary of Hopkins's experiments in a form of
versification known as "sprung rhythm."[12] Mimetically, the poem mirrors its
subject, being "dappled" in its syntax and "fickle" in its lexicon. Indeed, in its
studied unconventionality, "Pied Beauty" is an insistent, if subtle, reminder that

praise is never simply unmediated expression of a graced insight, but a matter of (in this case, exquisite) craft.

Read as commentary on praise in the form of praise, Hopkins's poem underscores a crucial insight: praise is not only language offered; it is also language *made*. This distinction between offering prayer and making poetry is vital to understanding praise as a rhetorical act. We can thus distinguish the "spontaneous yearning" identified by Foster as the essential spark of adoration from the more motivationally complex activity of praise as a specific rhetorical enactment of an adoring stance.

So stylistically rich is "Pied Beauty," beyond any strictly communicative purpose, that its poetry can be seen to compete with prayer. It draws attention to itself as both theological argument and verbal artistry at least as much as it serves as a vehicle by which its author or its readers may engage God, only obliquely addressed in the poem. Indeed, it is easy to read "Pied Beauty" as a poem whose subject is prayer rather than as a prayer in poetic dress. A more sympathetic reading might see in "Pied Beauty" an impulse to transcendence in its zeal to pair formal beauty with formal beauty. If imitation is the sincerest form of flattery, might Hopkins's efforts be understood to honor God through poetic representation of God's material handiwork?

Although, upon closer examination, the poem might be considered atypical of prayer, our brief encounter with it suggests no easy correspondence between an attitude of reverence and its formal manifestation as praise; indeed, "Pied Beauty" reveals a site of tension between these motives. Prayer may be a rhetoric in quest of perfected motives, but it is manifested in imperfect discourse, in language and bodily performance.

These motivational complexities are readily found in the spurned rhetoric of lament—the rhetorical counterpart to praise. The charge of being ill used by God or the gods ranks among the most profound and unsettling of prayers. "My God, my God, why have you forsaken me?" (Matt. 27:46), exclaims Jesus on the Cross, echoing the first verse of Psalm 22. U.S. playwright Tony Kushner tests how far a frame of prayer may be stretched, charging God with neglect, if not outright malevolence, in allowing the scourge of AIDS.[13] Kushner concludes his lengthy prayer with words of admonition: "At present we are homeless, or imagine ourselves to be. Bleeding life in the universe of wounds. Be thou more sheltering, God. Pay more attention" (224). Such prayer as this is a profound statement of distress, even anger, but it is also one of profound dependence, in sharp contrast with the irreverent stance parodied in the political cartoon at the beginning of this chapter. Demanding that God *be* God, even in rebuke, can be an act of profound reverence.

Despite its vehemence, Kushner's "AIDS Prayer" is not, to my ear, an act of arrogance, even as it pushes against the bounds of propriety. Kushner acknowledges this impropriety: "If prayer is a beseeching, a seeking after the hidden heart and face of God, then this peremptory, querulous, insistent demanding, this pounding at your door cannot be called a prayer, this importunate sleeve-tugging while you are distracted—concerned, perhaps with something more important, holding the earth to its orbit, perhaps, keeping it from careening into the sun: or perhaps you tend another world other than ours, and do a better job with that one, where there is nothing like AIDS, and your tutelage is gentler, and the lessons are easier to learn" (223). The Old Testament offers ample testimony of Israel (whose root means "striving or wrestling with God") speaking to God through bargain, protest, and lament.[14] From the beginning, this is a relationship marked by covenant and conflict, one in which reverence assumes many forms. Kushner's rhetoric sits recognizably within a tradition of lament. Walter Brueggemann notes that this tradition finds its warrant in the Book of Psalms with its numerous psalms of lament. When one considers that the same person or community may utter words of a similar spirit to those voiced by Hopkins, at one time, and by Kushner, at another, it becomes clear that these twin rhetorics of praise and accusation frame a complex terrain for the performance of reverence.

Praise has a second counterpart in its complement, petition. Lament resembles petition, with lament oriented toward what has happened and petition, toward what might happen. Petition is often regarded as synonymous with prayer, whereas praise is recognized as a mode of address in its own right. In one framing, praise is the culmination of the more elementary stage represented by petition; its outstretched branches are a mature expression of spiritual sensibility (it takes little imagination to see an upraised hand or angry fist in one of those branches). A return to the earthly humility of petition from the elevated language of praise can be regarded as acceptance of a fundamental condition of dependence. Together, praise and petition constitute a dynamic cycle, each a distinct manifestation of an attitude of reverence.

This image of a tree provides an occasion to consider an important connection between human and natural phenomena in a split running through prayer that would place petition on one side and praise on the other. As we saw in chapter 2, the scene of prayer depends on the projection of human capacities for language onto divine agents. Prayer is a human activity, not a divine one. However, in an image of a tree "reaching" upward in prayer, something in nature is imagined to perform an act of worship. Far from idiosyncratic conceits, such images are deeply conventional; they signal that the primary concern of praise is proper alignment within an ordered cosmos.

We can consider the insights into the nature of praise and the praise of nature by examining one of its clearest expressions:

> Praise the LORD from the earth, you sea monsters and all deeps,
> Fire and hail, snow and frost, stormy wind fulfilling his command!
> Mountains and all hills, fruit trees and all cedars!
> Wild animals and all cattle, creeping things and flying birds!
> Kings of the earth and all peoples, princes and all rulers of the earth!
> Young men and women alike, old and young together! (Psalms 148:7–12)

Together with other "praise" psalms (146–150), Psalm 148 forms a doxological conclusion to the Book of Psalms. This second, or "earthly," part of the psalm strongly echoes the ascent of earthly Creation, as recounted in Genesis, from primitive forces of nature, exemplified by sea monsters and other denizens of the deep, through a range of flora and fauna, to humans. The earthly orders of Creation are exhorted by the psalmist to "praise the LORD." These six verses follow six in which all celestial orders of Creation—Sun, Moon, stars, the angels and heavenly hosts, the highest heavens and beyond—are likewise commanded to praise the glory and majesty of the Lord. Nothing in Creation is excluded from this call to praise, framed by an opening and closing "Praise the LORD."

The third and final part of the psalm reaffirms the Lord's absolute sovereignty over all Creation: "Let them praise the name of the LORD, for his name alone is exalted; his glory is above earth and heaven" (v. 13). Read as an ideological statement, Psalm 148 articulates a sociopolitical vision of Israel's unique position in an unfolding divine plan: any "false" worship of lower orders of Creation that may linger is rhetorically undercut by images of harmony and unison, all eyes and voices cast in the same direction. There is no one properly to praise but the Lord. This exhortation to praise by the psalmist functions recognizably as a trope, not because the heavens and the Earth are imagined as capable of giving praise, but because the command to praise is a figure of apostrophe. All Creation, the psalmist understands, already renders the form of praise proper to its nature. The real focus of the prayer is on Israel, as becomes clear in the final verse: "He has raised up a horn for his people, praise for all his faithful, for the people of Israel who are close to him. Praise the LORD!" (v. 14). Israel is thus summoned to join the chorus of Creation in completion of a divine plan.

Psalm 148 may also be read as a portrait of reluctant participants in a cosmic drama, who must overcome their present estrangement from that natural drama by the *making* of praise. For human beings, praise is no longer a natural, spontaneous expression, but deliberate work. These matters of effort and estrangement from a natural state are much at issue in the rhetoric of praise. For praise may be understood not only as natural expression of gratitude or awe—a mirror to divine glory—but also as *language* (the form of praise proper to human beings) to convey what is due to the divine. Implicit in this psalm is an insight that praise must be reclaimed through the resources of art (poetry, music, dance). Human praise is not merely a matter of expression but, crucially, of invention. It is, in a word, rhetorical.

Though a distinction between nature and art is one easily taken for granted, the psalmist's implicit equation of artistic and natural praise opens up this distinction to closer examination, for it goes to the heart of prayer. As in the poetry of Hopkins, elements of artistic form are intimately bound up with the performance of praise. Yet Hopkins does not join nature in praise so much as complete (or compete with) the work of nature *through* praise, by giving human voice to the grandeur of God as manifested in Creation. In this understanding of praise, human beings are conceived as partners, even rivals, in an ongoing act of creation. Implicit in the psalmist's call for Israel to join with all Creation in a chorus of praise is a desire to transcend the limitations of language to achieve a state of perfect communication. Burke identifies this state as "pure persuasion," or "the farthest one can go, in matters of rhetoric" (*RM* 267). By contrast with the uncertain voice of language, wordless modes of expression such as music, dance, or the visual arts may take one further toward communion with the divine. So may silence, in which attention replaces speech, and time replaces words as prayer's currency. In this respect, the blast of the shofar that concludes Psalm 148 and the mute praise of the supplicant's prostrate body can be more eloquent modes of prayer than articulate speech.

Of all modes of prayer, then, praise provokes the greatest measure of anxiety, for it is the performance most open to charges of inadequacy and insincerity. By design, psalms and other formal prayers strive to bridge turbulent channels and to forestall anxieties that, left to the imagination, prayer would appreciably amplify.

Notwithstanding the use of textual and oral formulas to make prayer easier, praise is fraught with far more challenge and complexity than a celebratory stance might first seem to admit. Indeed, the very enthusiasm that accompanies efforts to praise and to exhort others to praise perversely signals those challenges. Were prayer not so difficult, far fewer models and methods would guide its practice. By comparison with other modes of prayer, in which one strives to accurately characterize one's situation, praise is discourse in *excess* of a specific situation; it is a language of hyperbole. Although prayer is anchored in a local context, praise transcends its specific moment to address a broader existential condition. Praise must be effusive, immoderate. Its performance is thus an anxious paradox: it must risk embarrassment in being too much since it cannot risk being insufficient or perfunctory.[15]

In *Blessed Excess*, Stephen H. Webb locates the essential trope of religion in hyperbole. Against the temperate and cautious rhetoric of modern intellectual thought, Webb advocates a rhetoric of glad abandonment. With Webb, I suggest that hyperbole, going too far, is the rhetorical figure of attitude, whether reverent or irreverent. Elsewhere, Webb characterizes hyperbole as "a vertical trope" whose purpose is "to see how far an observation can be taken when stripped of all reservation and qualification" (*Re-figuring* 88). Hyperbole apprehends the "vertical" distance between human speakers and divine addressees and seeks to overcome it: "By going too far, hyperbole is just right; its excess is just enough" (Webb *Blessed Excess* 20).

One measure of praise's hyperbolic character is its translation of response to a particular situation into responsibility, understood as emergent obligation.[16] Praise begets praise as an inscribed strategy for reading situations. Embedded in a regulative frame of liturgical scripts, the urgency of praise is tempered by tradition and codified into custom. Thus does inspiration accede to strategy, as adoration passes from the immediacy of speech into the mediated performance of song.

Only by becoming "coached" into ritual is reverence a fully human expression of whatever divine spark served as its initial inspiration. Here we return to the domain of poetry, in this case, poetry as a practical, even quotidian art. This is prayer as "equipment for living," to cite Burke's characterization of the proverbial, character-building dimension of the poetic acts (*PLF* 293). Herein lies the most profound source of anxiety surrounding praise: its artificial and replicable character. Praise becomes, in a word, routine. As Burke further observes in "Literature as Equipment for Living," when "situations are typical and recurrent in a given social structure, people develop names for them, and strategies for handling them," and he identifies such strategies precisely as "attitudes" (*PLF* 296–97).

Yet strategies to what end? Praise is language built up into a rhetoric of display. Its elaborate character—literally, it has been worked out—reveals praise to be a form of epideictic speech crafted for effect on an audience. It strives to please both by being true and by being beautiful. These objectives make praise a dangerous form of speech insofar as original revelation risks becoming hollowed out. When this in fact occurs, praise becomes nostalgic discourse marked as cliché and mere hyperbole. At such times, new language, set to new music, is necessary to reestablish a scene of excess, for praise is not only a response of excess; it is also a response *to* excess. The object of praise is perceived *as* excess, whether of power or some other virtue. The hyperbole of praise is a mimetic representation of its addressee. Although the possibility of failure to match rhetorical excess with real excess is ever present, this possibility is also the source of prayer's dynamism. The potential for failure is the ultimate guarantor of praise. *Unless* praise is difficult, it cannot be performed.

But what of joyous rhetoric that bespeaks a degree of ease in praise? What are we to make of it? To help us in this regard, we can consider the Magnificat, from the Gospel of Luke:

> My soul proclaims the greatness of the Lord, my spirit rejoices in God
>   my Saviour;
> He has looked with favour on his lowly servant.
> From this day all generations will call me blessed;
> The Almighty has done great things for me and holy is his name.
> He has mercy on those who fear him, from generation to generation.
> He has shown strength with his arm and has scattered the proud in their
>   conceit,
> Casting down the mighty from their thrones and lifting up the lowly.
> He has filled the hungry with good things and sent the rich away empty.
> He has come to the aid of his servant Israel, to remember his promise
>   of mercy,
> The promise made to our ancestors, to Abraham and his children for
>   ever. (1:46–55, ELLC)

Mary's greeting to her kinswoman Elizabeth serves to clarify and round out this chapter's portrait of praise. First, the prayer's seemingly effortless fluency is not a natural expression, but a studied performative pose. This Canticle of Mary is an idealized portrait of how praise might be imagined if performed under ideal conditions such as the inspiration of the Holy Spirit. Indeed, its eloquence mirrors the miraculous intervention that has brought children to each of these women, one a virgin, the other well past childbearing age. The Magnificat has been regarded in Christian tradition as "the perfect act of humility" and Mary herself the superlative model of a servant, or handmaiden, at prayer (Hardon).

Mary's words bear the mark of what Wordsworth would call "the spontaneous overflow of powerful feelings," later "recollected in tranquillity" (21); they bespeak an eloquence and wisdom far beyond her station or age. In this hymn, the inspiration attributed to Mary is owing to the disciplined labor of the Evangelist Luke, whose setting of these words is, according to tradition, divinely inspired. Echoing the psalms, the Magnificat is poetry embedded in text and tradition, yet receptive to inspiration. The eloquence embodied by praise is thus imagined as a surplus of rhetorical action or as invention aided by inspiration. This is prayer's enabling conceit in Christian tradition, "for we do not know how to pray as we ought, but that very Spirit intercedes with sighs too deep for words" (Rom. 8:26). Understanding prayer as a work of the heart completed through inspiration is akin to notions of the creative muses who inspire poetry, dance, and other arts. Paradoxically, success in praise comes at high cost; for unless a measure of humility intervenes, the scene in which such address is performed risks being made idolatrous or totemic by the performance of praise itself. Ultimately, praise is impossible without surrendering to the impossibility of the task.

The dynamic relation between labor and inspiration in praise and other modes of prayer invites scrutiny insofar as it raises questions about *agency* and *attitude* as conflicting motives, setting rhetorical competence against rhetorical insufficiency. Except as an enabling conceit, there can be no pure attitude, just as there can be no pure scene or pure act. Reverence, complexly manifested in the discourse of praise, is a fitting name for a fusion of motives, with attitude as a common denominator. To see where reverence may yet lead in apprehending prayer as rhetorical performance, let us turn to an instance of prayer in which praise is only one rhetorical move among many in a complex performance.

Reverence Beyond Praise: Mystery and Hierarchy

Although few would disagree that a profound irreverence marks much human interaction, a capacity for reverence is nonetheless "built in" to our socialization through language. Prayer stands out precisely in being a discursive space where reverence is given full expression. We can imagine a world drained of reverence, but not for long. More easily, we can imagine a cosmos depopulated of divine beings and a culture in which reverence is manifested toward the wrong objects. We detect an impulse toward reverence in ourselves and in others, whatever its objects. This impulse finds its logical summation in acts of address. And prayer, as I have argued, is its fullest, socialized expression.

To see how this is so, consider the following text:

> Welcome, o Supernatural One, o Swimmer,
> who returns every year in this world
> that we may live rightly, that we may be well.
> I offer you, Swimmer, my heart's deep gratitude.
>
> I ask that you will come again,
> that next year we will meet in this life,
> that you will see that nothing evil should befall me.
> O Supernatural One, o Swimmer, now
> I will do to you what you came here for me to do.
>   (Qtd. in Hirshfield 195)

This "Prayer to the Sockeye Salmon" by a Kwakiutl woman was transcribed and translated into English in 1895 by fellow Kwakiutl George Hunt in collaboration with anthropologist Franz Boas. The version of the text presented here is anthologized in Jane Hirshfield, ed., *Women in Praise of the Sacred*, "spiritual" writings by women drawn from multiple traditions and historical eras. It speaks eloquently to the indispensable role played by the sockeye in their annual spawning cycle in the life of First Nations of the Pacific Northwest. Because of the salmon's historic and still vital role as a principal food source, the stance of the speaker in this ritualized greeting before the annual kill is one of deep reverence toward the salmon for their willing sacrifice.

As gracious acknowledgment of dependence on the Sockeye, this ritual address articulates a recurring moment in an ongoing drama of sacrifice and survival, one in which the Kwakiutl and the Sockeye are implicated in a relationship where each play a crucial role. Every year, the Sockeye return as a life-giving offering. Mindful of this act of generosity, the Kwakiutl partake of the offering, ensuring "that [they] may live rightly, that [they] may be well." The prayer beautifully illustrates that reverence is necessarily speakable in a language of address. Thus the relationship between the Kwakiutl and the Sockeye is as discursive (at least on the part of the Kwakiutl) as it is material. The Kwakiutl do not simply experience reverent thoughts or feel gratitude toward this source of sustenance; they do not only speak reverently about the Sockeye in narrative. Their speech is also directed toward the Sockeye as appropriate addressee for an experience of gratitude. Reciprocally, the Sockeye are called upon to remember their duty.

A naive reading sees in this address an act of worship to a salmon god. Such was my own first encounter with this text. Its presence among other hymns in an anthology of praise did not discourage this reading. However, the particular setting for this performance proves crucial for understanding a sophisticated rhetorical transaction. According to Kwakiutl lore, the Salmon are a race of people living in five villages—one for each of five major species of salmon native to the Pacific Northwest—accessible only from under the sea. Every year, the Salmon People assume their fish form to travel upstream past Kwakiutl villages. This particular address is a ritual welcoming of the first, or leader, of the Salmon People taken in the annual fishing cycle. The salmon is not immediately killed, only stunned by a single blow; still alive, it may be addressed in words of respect so that it (or its spirit) may return to tell the Salmon People about the good treatment it has received.

The original account of this exchange as recorded in Boas's *Ethnology of the Kwakiutl* makes clear that the ritual utterance on which the anthologized prayer is based is offered by a woman acting in cooperation with her husband: "As soon as [the husband] arrives at the beach, his wife goes to meet him; and when she sees what has been caught by her husband, she begins to pray to it. The woman says, as she is praying: 'O Supernatural Ones! O, Swimmers! I thank you that you are willing to come to us. Don't let your coming be bad, for you come to be food for us. Therefore, I beg you to protect me and the one who takes mercy on me, that we might not die without cause, Swimmers!' Then the woman herself replies, 'Yes,' and goes up from the bank of the river" (Boas 609). This explanation reveals a social dimension to communication between different kinds of beings. The Sockeye, living in villages much of the year, but traveling to reproduce as fish, are seen to mirror the Kwakiutl.

The context presented allows for a reading of the yearly ritual less as worship than as a rhetorical exchange accompanying an economic exchange. Indeed, two different scenes of address may to said to operate at the same time: an act of gratitude for blessings received but also a game in which the Sockeye are tricked (by being well treated) into returning en masse. These accounts, each profound in its way, are complementary. One exalts and the other plays down the kill on which survival is based. To understand this ritual as a scene of reverent speech, we can discount neither of these readings.

What if the Kwakiutl decided *not* to welcome the Sockeye? Would they not come anyway? Skeptical critics of this address before the kill might observe that it is immaterial to whether the salmon return. It has only to do with the Kwakiutl's attitude toward the salmon run. Positioned as outsiders, we can read this address as an apostrophe and see its functions as normative for Kwakiutl society. Yet the address perfectly manifests at its most encompassing an indispensable attitude on the part of the Kwakiutl toward the arrival of the Sockeye. In other words, this experience of profound dependence is most fully realized in verbal terms that perfect the nonverbal situation. Only in reverent address is the actual situation in which Kwakiutl people find themselves fully realized.

For this address to occur, the Sockeye must be conceived as suitable addressees, invested with speech and related attributes of consciousness, intentionality, and power. A belief that the Sockeye mirror the Kwakiutl is one way to characterize their linguistic consubstantiality. Yet the impetus to do so comes not from any revelation that Sockeye exist or possess certain capabilities, but from an experience of dependence on which reverence is constructed. This attitude finds its outlet in address. The Sockeye are not addressed because they are imagined as people; they are imagined as people because they are addressed. Reverent address to the Sockeye dramatizes the motivational base—scene, act, attitude, agent, agency, and purpose all together—that enables discourse to bridge categorical divides between the human and the otherworldly. Whereas a scene of address as shared linguistic substance makes prayer possible, an attitude of reverence makes prayer *necessary*. Indeed, prayer's necessity allows for its possibility, and both arise from recognition of a fundamental condition of dependence.

As much as a relationship between the Kwakiutl and the Sockeye is figured in words, its ground goes beyond language. Whether this particular source of sustenance ought to be addressed is immaterial, for the Sockeye enjoy a stubborn material importance that undergirds any dramatic formulation. No prayer addresses beings deemed insubstantial. The Sockeye are no abstraction, even if a race of Salmon People depends on a literary projection of human social relationships onto a natural world. When the Kwakiutl address the Sockeye, they address the reality of a vital source, not a character in a story. What is true of this particular object of address is true more generally. The scene of prayer is an experience of something real on which one vitally depends. Though stories may be generated, divine beings do not begin as characters: before stories, before predication, they are encountered as realities to which response is owed. When that response performs an attitude of reverence, a scene of prayer comes into being.

Coda: In Search of Reverence

What can one say about a capacity for reverence that is not, finally, an argument for reverence? Descriptive ambition extends only so far before it becomes apparent that one *has* an attitude, reverent or irreverent, toward reverence. An account of how reverence comes to be (or comes to be lacking) cannot help but be a search for reverence in its multiple guises. To write about prayer and its situations, scenes, addresses, and attitudes, exposes one to charges of favoring, if not actually engaging in, the demystification of prayer's enabling conceits or of exposing its performative logic. The question at issue, then, in this or any account of prayer is whose *logos*—whose "-logy"—is basic? Is it theology? Sociology? Psychology? Biology? I make the case here for rhetoric as a praxis that pulls various these various *logoi* into productive relation.

Let me say here that I am *for* reverence in much the same way that a lover of poetry is for beauty or a philosopher for truth. Any project that so thoroughly considers prayer as a rhetoric is necessarily *for* something in prayer. I believe rhetoric is uniquely able to account for the principles of orientation that motivate reverence and that contribute to restoring reverence as an active principle in human affairs. Being for reverence begins in acknowledging its absence and negation. By "absence," I mean a discernible loss in the capacity to "dance" this attitude, individually or collectively, as a response to the situations in which we find ourselves. By "negation," I refer to abundant instances of irreverence, from the mocking, deprecating stance of satire to broader tendencies to regard other persons and things as mere extensions of ourselves. Irreverence denies its ethical responsibility to the other. It disrespects hierarchies as a matter of principle.

In contrast, the humor to be found in pillorying an irreverent reverend begins in a sensibility that would see the pretentious brought down to size. It embraces hierarchy as an instinctive regard for ordered relations—everything in its proper place. Humor leads to the deeper insight that a lampooned figure stands in need of prayer in a scene of antiprayer that makes objects of others—in Buber's terms, Paisley's "You" is addressed as an "It," not as a "Thou." Consonant with

Burke's "spirit of hierarchy," reverence is oriented upward and committed to the rightness of some set of ordered relations (*LASA* 15). But what is to be made of how the impulse to reverence can contribute to ethical engagement? If reverence is, in Burkean terms, a "frame of acceptance" of an existing hierarchy (or one whose arrival is welcomed), it is also one that finds its natural expression in a language of address (*ATH* 5). If we consider some situation of fundamental dependence, as between the Kwakiutl and the Sockeye, but remove any possible linguistic connection, what do we have?

I suggest that what we have is our present situation with respect to many relationships—with people, objects, abstractions, and the world as a whole. Without a rhetorical situation in which an attitude of reverence may be performed in discourse, there can be no prayer. Is reverence possible absent divine beings or in contexts other than prayer? This is among the most pressing of unaddressed rhetorical questions.

The emergence of reactionary fundamentalisms and a parallel emergence of new religious movements centered in environmentalism and empowerment may be read as fractured efforts to hold onto the sacred in a universe depopulated of compelling objects of address, one where the range of possible audiences has contracted considerably. We have yet to absorb the shock of this contraction in spiritual diversity. Insofar as one embraces the paradigms of modern science or is engulfed by the insistent demands of an increasingly globalized economy, a capacity for reverence in prayer of some kind is increasingly open to challenge. We must ask where reverence goes, if not into prayer or worship? In the absence of divine beings, to what other audiences can we express gratitude, acknowledge profound dependence, and stand in awe? If reverence, upward address, is essential to a meaningful life, do we not therefore require scenes of prayer?

It is impossible to know what forms of reverence will survive or replace the loss of the sacred as it has been known. It is hard to imagine the survival of the Salmon People in an era of commercial canneries, dammed rivers, and industrial-scale aquaculture. Yet they do survive even now, not only in stories but also in scenes whose ritual enactment counteracts forces that threaten the Kwakiutl way of life. These practices serve indispensably as modes of cultural memory binding generations into communities of practice over time. If, with Burke, we believe prayer epitomizes the perduring functions of rhetoric, we might conclude that prayer will persist, even as theological conceptions of divine beings evolve. It seems safe to predict that new principles of orientation, new pieties, will emerge from the dialectic of novelty and nostalgia.

Because all the elements of prayer are deeply implicated in our nature as social and linguistic beings, our capacity for reverence cannot be separated from it. Reverence is no less linguistic than social. In *A Rhetoric of Motives*, Burke offers "mystery" as a phenomenological term for what I have located in "reverence." "Mystery," he asserts "arises at that point where different kinds of beings are in communication. In mystery there must be strangeness; but the estranged must also be thought of as in some way capable of communion" (115). Mystery extends across all categorical divisions to find its ultimate reach in the theological realm, where the differences between kinds of entities in communication are most pronounced. For Burke, persuasion and identity are intimately bound with mystery:

> (1) Persuasion is a kind of communication. (2) Communication is between different things. (3) But difference is not felt merely as between *this* entity and *that* entity. Rather, it is felt realistically, as between *this kind* of entity and *that kind* of entity. (That is, communication between entities becomes communication between *classes* of entities.) (4) A persuasive communication between kinds (that is, persuasion by identification) is the abstract paradigm of *courtship*. Such appeal, or address, would be the technical equivalent of love. (5) But courtship, love, is "mystery." For love is a communion of estranged entities, and strangeness is a condition of mystery. (176–77, emphasis in original)

In a formulation that imagines prayer as the perfection of the rhetorical principle, Burke compresses rhetoric's character as *scene* ("*this* entity and *that* entity"), *act* ("courtship") and *attitude* ("love," "mystery") into a dense "logical" sequence. Indeed, a page later, Burke explicitly identifies prayer as the "ultimate reach of communication between different classes of beings" performed with an attitude of "reverent beseechment" (*RM* 178).

For Burke, mystery is a free-floating principle, "inevitable in systematic thought" and inherent in relationships of all sorts (*RM* 141). It fixes on elements in the "social hierarchy" because prayer, even in its "pure" form requires an appropriate object (179). "One cannot without an almost suicidal degree of perfection merely pray," Burke explains. "One must pray *to something*" (179, emphasis in original). The hierarchical principle is a linguistic structure implicit in the relationship of things as ordered. For Burke, the final element of any ordered list is not merely itself, but also the perfection of that list—what Burke characterizes as a "terministic compulsion" to take things as far as they can go (*LASA* 19).

Reverence in prayer can be regarded as the perfection of a principle that allows for "respectful pleading" in all social relationships. Divine beings thus preside over a state of relations and embody principles that hold it together. For instance, love between persons different in kind (mother and child, male and female) or entities made consubstantial through a transcendent category (guild, tribe) rises to a level of principle to guarantee the character of an experience. Thus is "Love" or "Brotherhood" or some other principle raised to a personification. The God of monotheism is an ever-expanding cluster of principles in and out of harmony. Mystery begins in the insight that those with whom we relate are not, finally, identical to ourselves, hence a rhetoric of consubstantiality to establish shared identity at the level of scene. And not merely different, but estranged, hence a desire to transcend division. This desire is realized most fully in praise addressed to an object of reverence, conceived as both other and the perfection of some principle, hence the love letter and the hymn. Such reverential acts rise and fall together as expressions of our deep socialization—a product of our linguistic embodiment.

In chapter 1, we saw that prayer is profitably understood as an alternative space of performance, a "rehearsal for living," where our rhetorical capacities are tested in anticipation of engaging others. This notion is akin to what Benedictine monks understand their motto "Ora et labora" (Pray and work) to mean— each activity is a purposeful effort that completes the other. The persistence of prayer across diverse spiritual habitats and diverse manifestations is testament to a felt need for reverence in responding to situations. Prayer's ultimate concern is the construction of character in ethical relation to others in light of our condition as materially constrained, linguistically embodied beings. The question, then, is what forms of reverence can fashion and maintain our social constitution as responsive and responsible beings? This is not, finally, the task of philosophy or even theology, I would argue, but of rhetoric since the forms of reverence are not immutable but ever adaptable to new contexts and discoverable only in performance.

As Debra Hawhee recounts in *Bodily Arts*, rhetoric, conceived as public oratory, was an embodied art, a complement to athletics and music in the classical era (13). As a species of rhetoric, or oratory in a particular sense, prayer is among the "arts of subject production" (14). This emphasis on character formation connects prayer's phenomenological and rhetorical, its affective and social dimensions.

Thus I have endeavored to present prayer as psychosomatic performance and reverence, its habitual attitude, as manifested in discursive performance. Like other attitudes, reverence mediates between agents and actions, between performance and character, building up structures of piety in individuals and communities. Reverence is experienced as a mystery whose presence opens up possibilities for rhetorical invention or inspiration. As both the "dancing" and the "coaching" of attitude, reverence attends a performance of address by and upon its performer, who, in expressing reverence toward some other, discovers a more secure and experientially true place to stand amid uncertainty. Yet the praying subject constituted in individual bodies, minds, and spirits is never an experiential monad. In moving outward from prayer centered in the mind and body of individuals to the mind and body of a community, my claim that prayer is a relational and social art performed in concert with others across time and space is perhaps the most contestable of the claims I offer here. Chapters 5 and 6 turn to prayer as a mediating and mediated discourse through interpretive lenses provided by classical rhetoric's canons of memory and delivery.

5

PERFORMING THE MEMORARE:
PRAYER AS A RHETORICAL ART OF MEMORY

This is the covenant that I will make with the house of Israel after those days, says the LORD: I will put my laws in their minds and write them on their hearts; and I will be their God, and they shall be my people.

—Hebrews 8:10

Those who cannot remember the past are condemned to repeat it.

—George Santayana, *The Life of Reason*

In choosing commercial greeting cards for loved ones, friends, and acquaintances on various occasions, we search for texts and images that encapsulate relations between ourselves and our intended recipients—as they are or how we might wish them to be. Greeting cards allow others to speak for us. Most of us accept the conventions that the cards can speak for us better than we can for ourselves, that they represent no breach of etiquette, and that neither uniqueness nor authenticity is expected on the occasions we normally use them. It little matters that others choose or receive identical cards. What matters is that we "stand behind" the words we borrow.

Greeting cards and prayer have much in common. Both manifest presence through material agency. Both depend on borrowed eloquence as a legitimate means for sharing thoughts and intentions. Indeed, prayer stands out for its reliance on scripts and models for the social relations it would foster. Prayer need not be unique or authentic or freshly composed at the moment of utterance to be genuine. Although models of extemporaneous prayer hold sway in certain communities of practice, all prayer depends on quotation of words and gestures. Even at its most spontaneous, it relies on genre knowledge to shape what to say and how to say it. It relies, in other words, on practices of *memory*.

This chapter approaches prayer as a rhetorical art of memory. I argue that prayer is shaped by cognitive, social, and material practices in its concerns with linkages within individual minds and across communities. These practices include the internalizing of prayer not only through memorization, but also through writing, reading, and meditating upon images. Thus, I further argue, prayer is not only address, invocation, reverence; it is also memory. Indeed, the rhetoric of prayer is lodged in memory, the fourth of classical rhetoric's canons. More than most discourse, prayer is about memory, the least understood and most dispersed of rhetoric's operations. Is memory the penultimate stage in the composing of speech before delivery? Or is memory a "stage" in a different sense—a platform for rhetorical performance? Does memory refer to activities taking place in individual minds or to cultural practices of storage, retrieval, and material signification?

Recently, Egyptologist Jan Assmann has identified religion as fertile ground for memory studies, an emergent discipline that engages linkages between cognition and culture. In *Religion and Cultural Memory*, Assmann posits two types of collective memory: "communicative memory," the "social aspect of individual memory" that exists "in the intermediary realm between individuals" (3) and a domain of affective experience centered in the body; and "cultural memory," located in texts, traditions, and institutions with and by which individuals and communities interact (8). Prayer operates at the intersection between communicative and cultural memory. As memory, prayer is at once cognitive and social, internal and external. Memory in prayer is manifested, above all, in *mindfulness*—our capacity to bring things into relationship.

Prayer and memory are close cognates under a heading of "socialized craft." As a craft centered in habits of recollection, prayer is largely indistinguishable from the socializing functions of memory; as a socialization of thought, memory, in turn, is a vital operation of prayer. Indeed, memory's multiple senses and prayer's diverse practices can be brought into surprising and satisfying alignment. This chapter presents a broad sketch of prayer in relation to memory with a particular focus on the role of text (borrowed words) in performing prayer as an act of individual and social, communicative and cultural memory. It approaches prayer as things remembered in individual bodies and in material practices, reading a single, appropriately titled prayer, the Memorare, as a touchstone for considering prayer's character as a socialized craft of memory.

Chapter 1 considered prayer in situational terms with a focus on kairos and krisis as ways of marking prayer as rhetorical response. Chapters 2 through 4 examined prayer in "motivational" terms using Burke's dramatistic tools of *scene*, *act*, and *attitude* to open prayer to rhetorical inquiry. These four chapters accounted for prayer as "*strategic* answers, *stylized* answers" to situations, "situa-tions" being "but another word for motives" (Burke *GM* 1, emphasis in original; *PC* 29); they identified linguistic and social dimensions of prayer as well as its embodied and material character. This chapter and the next round out the rhetoric of prayer—an interweave of spirit and matter—by considering how prayer is localized by practices of memory and *transmitted* by acts of delivery. Memory and delivery are thus conceived as dimensions of performance that ground prayer's spiritual concerns in the cognitive, social, and material aspects of discourse.

A focus on memory as spiritual embodiment follows appropriately from a focus on prayer as attitude, even as it shifts from a Burkean dramatistic critical lens to a traditional, canonical one. As our look at the dialogue between prayer and traditional rhetoric's forgotten canons will make clear, memory and deliv-ery are as ripe for revaluation as prayer is.

The "Aboutness" of Prayer: Motives of Memory and Desire

That prayer is about memory on some level is easily enough confirmed. Prayer is a primary vehicle of commemoration, mediating the past to serve the present. In prayer, persons and events are called to mind, made present so that they may be prayed over. Liturgical prayer, especially, is a performance of cultural mem-ory. Notably, the Catholic Mass is a complex memorial act, including its center-piece, the Eucharistic Prayer (or Great Thanksgiving), celebrating the death and resurrection of Jesus Christ. Citing Jesus, this prayer reiterates the authorizing words of institution: "Do this in memory of me" (Luke 22:19, NAB). Liturgy (Greek *leitourgia*, or "work of the people") is at once a collection, a gathering of persons, and a *re*collection, a calling to mind through prayer.

Prayer originates from the matrix, or "womb," of memory, a matrix located, alternatively, in the mind or in the heart: "This is the covenant that I will make with the house of Israel after those days, says the LORD: I will put my laws in their minds and write them on their hearts; and I will be their God, and they shall be my people" (Heb. 8:10). This notion of God's law as written on the heart appears several places in the Bible (Jeremiah 31:33; Hebrews 8:10) as a compel-ling metaphor linking memory and devotion. This image of inscription under-scores the covenant between God and Israel represented in the commandments given to Moses, famously inscribed on two stone tablets. The New Testament

Epistle to the Hebrews here echoes the Old Testament book of Jeremiah in its oblique reference to violation of the covenant through disobedience. No longer can the permanency of text set in stone be presumed, now that the tablets of the Law (as a material manifestation of the covenant) have been destroyed. In a new covenant, the Law will be inscribed on more receptive material, the heart, notwithstanding the irony that mortal flesh is far less durable than stone. Mind and heart, the implication is clear, offer more promising sites for inscription in representing embodied receptiveness to the word of God.

The claim that prayer is fundamentally about memory is not without its complications. Prayer is at least much the domain of desire as memory. Opening his *Confessions*, Saint Augustine proclaims, "You have made us for yourself, O Lord, and our heart is restless until it rests in you" (1.1.1). In a text conceived as both desiring prayer and searching memory, Augustine voices a key insight that memory nurtures desire, informs its inchoate yearnings. Augustine's pilgrimage to a place of rest is a return to origins accomplished by memory.

In recent commentary on *Confessions*, historian Garry Wills proposes that its Latin title, *Confessiones*, is properly translated "Testimony" (*Childhood* 13–15).[1] This change highlights *Confessions'* memorial character since testimony, an act of witness, involves a performance of memory. Indeed, after devoting nine books of *Confessions* in prayerful address to God, informed by memory, Augustine turns, in book 10, to the faculty of memory itself. Memory, for Augustine, is a "vast and unlimited inner chamber" containing virtually the whole world of sense perceptions and affections (10.8.15). Augustine's metaphor subtly contrasts cavernous and capacious notions of memorial space, things lost to memory and things found by virtue of method, in this case, the mnemotechnic "method of loci" (Yates).[2] He poignantly addresses both God and the fear of forgetting: "How then shall I find you, if I do not remember you?" (10.17.26).[3] He recognizes the possibility of being adrift in a sea of memory, an abundance of disconnected events and random images, absent a principle of orientation to shape memories into a coherent narrative. *Confessions* is Augustine's effort to explore the vast recesses of mind—his own and that of others—guided by a divine lodestar. Prayer, Augustine realizes, is discourse in dynamic relation with memory's backward and desire's forward impulses.

Whatever urgencies animate address to the divine, whatever experiences of awe inspire a reverent impulse in the human soul, prayer's energies are channeled by forces of tradition or, in other words, the things that have been handed down. Prayer proceeds not only by channeling inner drives in response to calls from without, but also by engaging the knowledge and values shared by a community, or what in rhetorical tradition has been understood as a *sensus communis*. More than "common sense," a sensus communis refers to things held in common. These are the common topics, or commonplaces, of social memory that connect ideas to ideas and minds to minds as the substance of any rhetorical appeal.[4]

Augustine's personal journey grounds prayer in individual memory and desire. At the same time, his interlacing of biography and biblical text demonstrates that communicative memory is ultimately inseparable from cultural memory. Prayer is discourse highly invested in the integration of memory's different scales. Indeed, as a craft of spiritual formation, prayer has very much to do with individual and collective bodies that remember, an observation that echoes chapter 4's discussion of prayer as the "coaching" of an attitude but with a shift of emphasis here from attitude to the material on which prayer may be said to work.

However tempting it may be to center any account of prayer and memory in the inexhaustible riches of Augustine's mind, it is in more quotidian settings that prayer as a devotional craft of memory is most apparent. Let us turn, therefore, to a prayer that anchors these initial speculations in concrete practice.

Praying the Memorare

The Memorare (Latin, "to remember") is a classic Marian prayer. Mention it to Catholics of a certain age and they will recite it for you and tell you instances when and where they have done so before. Addressed to Mary, Mother of God, the prayer descends from a fifteenth-century Latin text (Thurston).[5] Though legend associates it with the twelfth-century Cistercian Saint Bernard of Clairvaux (1090–1153), liturgical scholars attribute the prayer to the seventeenth-century French cleric Père Claude Bernard (1588–1641). Beyond the accident of similar names, the practice of attaching popular prayers to major saints is quite common. Thus the familiar "Prayer of Saint Francis" dates back to the early twentieth century, not to the thirteenth century of Saint Francis of Assisi. According to historian Herbert Thurston, Père Bernard popularized this prayer in French and other vernacular languages in his ministry to the indigent and incarcerated of Paris. Bernard, who claimed to have learned the prayer from his father, is said to have distributed over two hundred thousand leaflets featuring his "Oraison à la Vierge" (Prayer to the Virgin). Like many Marian prayers, his was associated with tales of remarkable physical cures and spiritual conversions, Bernard himself claiming to have been a beneficiary of its miraculous powers.

In the centuries after Bernard's evangelizing, the Memorare became well established among the cultic prayers to Mary, a collection that includes the Salve Regina, the Angelus, and, most notably, the various prayers of the Rosary.[6] It achieved canonical status in 1846 following its inclusion (as prayer 339) in the papally sanctioned *Raccolta: or Collection of Indulgenced Prayers.*[7] In the latter half of the nineteenth century, the Memorare only increased in popularity, especially in Ireland, whence it spread to the New World and beyond with the Irish diaspora. Through the 1970s, the Memorare remained among a handful of prayers whose observance marked popular Catholic piety. It may still be found in most collection of Catholic prayers and is commonly featured on devotional prayer cards. Such "holy cards," or *immaginette* (Italian, "little images"), are an expression of vernacular religious literacy as well as "rich repositories of personal and cultural memory" (George and Salvatori 250).

Prayer cards are similar in function to secular greeting cards, with the former recited by performers in devotional settings and the latter read by recipients in secular settings. Using a holy card as a multimodal tool for entering a scene of prayer, one can meditate on an image of the Virgin on the front side and recite the Memorare printed on the other:

> Remember, O Most Gracious Virgin Mary
> That never was it known
> That anyone who fled to thy protection,
> Desired your help or sought your intercession was left unaided.
> Inspired by this confidence,
> We fly unto you,
> O virgin of virgins, our mother,
> To you we come, before you we kneel,
> Sinful and sorrowful.
> O Mother of the Word Incarnate
> Despise not our petitions
> But in your mercy hear and answer us. (Griffin 81–82)

Though short, the text is rich and rewards attention. In keeping with tradition, it receives its title from its opening word, "Memorare" (used here as an imperative: "Remember"). Like other prayers to Mary, it is invocation recognizing her as a figure of holiness, protection, and consolation, befitting her nature as Mother of God. This particular invocation takes the form of a highly stylized petition reminding Mary of her beneficent intercession.

The prayer explicitly calls on Mary to do two things: to "remember" her response to those who have appealed to her; and to "hear and answer" present petitions. Performing the prayer, the petitioner beseeches Mary to intercede with Jesus. (Mary and all other saints are understood to exercise an intercessory, rather than instrumental, role.) What is significant, however, is that Mary is nowhere in the text recognized as an intercessor. The only parties represented are earthly petitioners and heavenly Mary. Most remarkable, perhaps, is the prayer's abstract character, for it is as devoid of specific supplications as it is replete with mannered invocations. The prayer stages a scene of supplication without petitioning for anything in particular. Its aim is to gain Mary's attention and good offices and, just as important, to remind the petitioner of Mary's constancy. Thus crafted, the Memorare is a text for a performance on emergent occasions, one that models an appropriate stance of entreaty. In dramatic terms, it serves as a script featuring roles for both performer and audience.

Notwithstanding its Christian cast, the argument of the prayer closely corresponds to appeals to other divine beings. Drawing on categories of prayer in the polytheism of ancient Greece, the Memorare may be classified by its explicit warrant: "Give because you have given" (in Greek: "Da quia dedisti"; Pulleyn 17). Its persuasive "hook" is the assertion that it is in the *nature* of Mary to serve in this mediating role. In many respects the feminine face of God in Christianity, Mary is addressed as the most fitting audience to which humans may communicate their most urgent concerns.

As its title indicates, the Memorare is an explicit reminder with a touch of intimidation. Even as it respectfully petitions, the prayer suggests that if Mary is who people say she is, she will hear this prayer as she has heard others in the past. With "never was it known . . . ," the Memorare recognizes that Mary's reputation is at stake. Calling on Mary to "remember" is an act of boldness, but it is boldness justified by tradition. That said, the Memorare also reflexively addresses its performers. In theological terms, Mary needs no reminder of her role within the realm of salvation. However, those who call upon her do require such reminders, if not specifically then more generally—to remind them of their place as suppliants before the Virgin Mary.

The Memorare underscores that recollection does not occur at the individual level only. This and similar prayers are performed as cultic acts in the context of cultural memory. To pray this prayer is to participate in a collective, ongoing act. Significantly, in the version of the prayer above, the speaking subject is figured in the plural: "to you we come," "before you we kneel," "our mother." The Memorare is imagined as a collective act. Whether performed in an individual or a communal setting, its scene of address is a collective one distributed over time. Where others have stood, "we" now stand, praying to Mary in the very same posture, the very same words. An imagined collectivity of persons unknown to one another prays this same prayer as a practice of cultural memory. For one prays the Memorare not as an individual but as a member of a faith community. In performing this prayer, one does not merely borrow words, one joins a dispersed chorus. Indeed, in the Memorare, the Church also remembers itself.

The prayer's dramatic appeal recalls Mikhail Bakhtin's concept of the *chronotope*, literally time-space, to refer to the "intrinsic connectedness of temporal and spatial relationships that are artistically expressed in literature" ("Forms of Time" 84). The Memorare manifests two "chronotopic" moments—the accumulating past of history ("never was it known") and the continuous present of supplication. Temporally, the prayer performs itself as *tradition*—something handed down in the past and, reciprocally, received in the present and to be received in the future. Others have prayed this prayer; others *will* pray this prayer. Spatially, the Memorare has its speakers both move through space ("We fly unto you") and repose in it ("before you we kneel").

Recognizing that one participates in a tradition is integral to performing this prayer: each iteration of the Memorare deposits a layer of tradition. Working in a Bakhtinian tradition, Paul Prior and Jody Shipka identify such layered activity as a "chronotopic lamination." Though they apply this notion of lamination to the *composing* of texts, it is productively extended to their cumulative reception and iterative performance. Within an oral or textual tradition, the performance of prayer is a laminated practice. Each iteration deepens that tradition and contributes to its internalization as communicative memory. This is memory informed by tradition and performed *as* tradition. What is external in cultural memory becomes embodied in communicative memory and vice versa.

The Memorare as Epitome, Prayer as Habitus

Our close reading of the Memorare has drawn out some of the ways memory operates in prayer. Although, despite its name, the Memorare does not much differ from other prayers as embedded cultural tradition and embodied devotional practice, its foregrounding of memory epitomizes prayer's memorial character.

First, the Memorare is fashioned to be *memorable* through the affordances of text: it simply cannot be understood apart from its materialization as text. This is true not only in its compositional structure, but also and especially in its mode of dissemination. Being a form of popular piety, the Memorare is relatively easy to learn (although other Marian prayers are easier still). As with many prayers in Christian tradition and beyond, it is typically first encountered through formal religious instruction and later committed to memory by repeated recitation. The Memorare is a prayer many learn to recite in communal devotion as children.

Once committed to memory, the prayer may be called into service as occasion warrants. The occasion need not be one of crisis, however. Despite its dramatic framing of importunity, the Memorare is largely regulative in function. Its gothic cadences manifest a scene of composure, one in which there is time for rhetorical amplification. In this respect, the prayer presents an idealized stance toward prayer's purpose and offers itself as a means for acquiring a proper perspective. In praying the Memorare, one internalizes the knowledge of what to do in an actual crisis.

Second, and a related point, the Memorare presents faithful practitioners with theological lessons ready to be internalized. This is the prayer's didactic function. Performing the Memorare contributes to one's spiritual formation. Internalized, this prayer, along with others, models relationships with the divine. Moreover, within Catholic tradition, one does not outgrow these elemental or formulary prayers. They hold their value even when one's spiritual repertoire expands to higher forms of prayer, such as meditation, and to extemporaneous performance. The genre knowledge that comes from mastering set prayers contributes to compositional skill in producing other prayers through imitation.

Third, the Memorare functions within a broader system of devotional observance, one that contributes to both the storing and the storying of prayer through the assembling of individual texts and practices into a greater whole. This is remembering as an act not of recall but of integration. What may be difficult to discern in focusing on any single prayer becomes apparent in a complete activity system of prayer. Here "activity system" is used in the sense advanced by cultural-historical activity theory to describe processes and contexts for social development, based on the findings of Russian psychologist Lev Vygotsky

(1896–1934).[8] Working within a Vygotskian paradigm, writing theorist David Russell defines an *activity system* as "any ongoing, object-directed, historically conditioned, dialectically structured, tool-mediated human interaction" (509). In this framework, prayer involves learning, performing, and sponsoring an activity and particular texts as the objects of that activity.

Indeed, prayers such as the Memorare are fully appreciated only through recall of extensive systems that structure individual and communal devotion within a *community of practice*. Approached in isolation, any prayer can seem unmoored. As part of a broader tradition to which it contributes, however, it both informs and is informed by its relationship to other prayers. Here "community of practice" is used in the sense advanced by anthropologists Jean Lave and Etienne Wenger to refer to "groups of people who share a concern or a passion for something they do and learn how to do it better as they interact regularly" (Wenger). Here the term refers to the cooperative character of prayer as an activity learned and performed by specific pray-ers. Of course, given that prayer's activities are often widely dispersed across space and time, prayer involves different kinds of communities of practice than are typically considered under notions of cooperative practices.

Fourth, the Memorare highlights the role of modality in prayer, in this case, the modality of text. Although the prayer dramatizes a scene of speech, it originates in a literate culture, as a product of writing. Here text facilitates the transmission of prayer within the communities where it circulates. Text memorializes prayer. Text and other modes of storage and retrieval extend a speaking body's communicative capacities and, what is important, allow for memory's externalization in material form, whether visible, audible, or tactile. Memory's externalization is essential for its socialization, as can be seen in material manifestations of cultural memory in physical sites like the Lincoln Memorial and in commemorative practices such as birthdays and other rites of passage. These material and social practices objectify memory.

So pervasive is prayer's interaction with material commonplaces of memory that it is impossible to conceive of prayer *without* texts, images, postures, sounds, smells, ambulatory circuits, and other memorial modalities. By design, these practices and objects prompt recollection and imagination in order to bring a performer into a scene of prayer. In this sense, memory serves as a "compositional art," one that, Mary Carruthers observes, is "involved with fostering the qualities we now revere as 'imagination' and 'creativity'" (*Craft* 9). In performing prayer, the rhetorical task is to take up the material of memory and perform it *into* a communicative act.

As a "treasure-house of inventions," *memoria* stood in dynamic relation to *inventio*, rhetoric's primary canon, Carruthers tells us in her magisterial *The Book of Memory*; its systematic practices played an incalculably important role in medieval culture, contributing to the building of "character, judgment, citizenship, and piety" through the "institutionalizing" of texts (11). These texts, Carruthers claims, "weave a community together by providing it with shared experience and a certain kind of language, the language of stories that can be experienced over and over again through time and as occasion suggests" (14). Although speaking generally about texts in medieval culture, she could be referring specifically to prayer, so accurately does she characterize its social functions.

Notions of memory as treasury, storehouse, and seedbed of invention continue to shape our understanding of the functions of memory—both in prayer and elsewhere. Carruthers offers another metaphor for memory: "Medieval *memoria* was a universal thinking machine, *machina memorialis*—both the mill that ground the grain of one's experiences (including all that one read) into a mental flour with which one could make wholesome new bread, and also the hoist or windlass that every wise master mason learned to make and to use in constructing new matters" (*Craft* 4). In linking memory to things mechanical, she makes the larger point that, as a craft, memory requires skill and expertise. To speak of prayer as a site of memory, then, is to move beyond scenes of rote learning and toward matters of craft and cooperative endeavor. In discussing monastic traditions of meditative prayer, Carruthers observes that memory is "not restricted to what we now call memory, but is a much more expansive concept, for it recognizes the essential roles of emotion, imagination, and cogitation within the activity of recollection" (2).

Prayer makes use of devotional practices both to store and to story memory. One such practice, typically performed in a church, is the Via Crucis, or Way of the Cross, in which devotees complete a circuit of the fourteen stations of Christ's crucifixion, stopping at each station (e.g., Station Ten—"Jesus is stripped of his garments") to meditate on Christ's Passion. By interacting with a visual representation of the biblical narrative to re-create the Way of the Cross and by moving physically through the process, one effectively performs oneself *into* this cultural memory. Through such chronotopic practices, time and space are transcended so that Christ's crucifixion is an event here and now, not only in a distant past. A related practice, though in a different idiom, is walking a labyrinth as a mode of meditative prayer in which the completion of a path inward and then outward constitutes a metaphorical spiritual journey.

A different systematic practice of memory is involved in the compilation of prayers into textual "treasuries," such as breviaries, psalters, and books of hours for use in private devotion or hymnals for use in public devotion. Notable among such systematic texts as a form of social memory is the Book of Common Prayer in Anglican tradition. Textual repositories serve a constitutive role as spiritual capital for a community of practice; they define what it is possible to say in prayer and thus shape a community's self-understanding. The localization of cultural memory in a traditional prayer book is a particular instance of a faith community's roots in sacred scripture. The Torah in Judaism, the Bible in Christianity, the Koran in Islam are each *the* memorial commonplace in their respective cultural traditions. But cultural memory need not be centered in texts. Oral transmission of myth (narrative) and a range of material practices are equally constitutive of memory.

Within certain scenarios, then, it is possible, and in some case even obligatory, to say a prayer previously composed by another, memorialized as text, and performed by others still. In these scenarios, prayer with borrowed words does not contravene the role of imagination and creativity, any more than performing music composed by others does. Indeed, when prayer is recognized as a collaborative act of social memory, the option or even the obligation to use borrowed words makes much sense. By far, the bulk of prayer uttered is formulary in both oral and written contexts. The activity of prayer requires that one both learn prayers and learn how to perform them properly.

This is not to suggest that "set" prayers are universally preferred over "spontaneous" prayer. Indeed, an emphasis on sincerity in prayer in Protestant tradition poses significant challenges to forms of cultural memory in traditions of received prayer. In the English Reformation, for example, the iconoclastic spirit arising among nonconformists against the use of set forms of prayer is notably expressed by John Milton: "This is evident, that they who use no set forms in prayer, have words from their affections; while others are to seek affections fit and proportionable to a certain doss of prepared words" (3.505). Here in the appropriately titled *Eikonoklastes* (image breaker), "set forms" are suspect, counterfeit, imposed from above, and a tyranny to be overthrown insofar as conformity to received prayer is an impediment to sincere, spontaneous, spirit-filled prayer. This understanding of prayer articulates a much different investment in memory and remains a counterpoint to more tradition-bound practices.

Fifth, and finally, images of bodies hastening toward Mary and kneeling before her in the Memorare verbally dramatize physical modes of performance. These images implicitly recognize prayer to be as much an embodied as a dis-cursive art. The Memorare attends to placement and posture as if Mary is to be approached not only spiritually but physically. In the fullest realization of this scene, entreating Mary is a multimodal, not merely a verbal, performance. The use of devotional images on holy cards to promote a spiritual encounter with Mary in visual as well as auditory terms is precisely what an iconoclastic impulse would object to. Even so, sacred images, rosary beads, and pious postures are as much a part of prayer's performative grammar as words are.

Thus images of the body in prayer point to a basic understanding of prayer as the training or conditioning of the embodied soul. Indeed, techniques for physical training for athletic contests in ancient Greece parallel those employed in teaching oratory, as Debra Hawhee documents in *Bodily Arts* (13). Prayer, as a species of oratory, is likewise a bodily art in which spiritual and physical comportment are intertwined. Indeed, prayer's mental and physical dimen-sions constitute a habitus. In chapter 4, I noted connections between *habitus*, a term made prominent by Pierre Bourdieu, and Burkean notions of attitude as "incipient action." In the present context, I further recognize a close association of habitus with the operations of memory.

Reading Bourdieu, Hawhee understands *habitus* to be "a system of disposi-tions that emerge in relation to structures and practices" (13). Prayer is very much a habitus, I would argue, one whose acquisition involves "rhythm, repeti-tion, and response" (Hawhee 13), akin to spiritual "muscle memory." Attention to habitus as "a socialized subjectivity" opens onto concerns about method for the cultivation of dispositions (Bourdieu and Wacquant 126). If, as I would further argue, prayer is a socialized craft for building up a properly devotional character prayer by prayer, then how best to achieve this outcome becomes most significant. For prayer is nothing if not methodical in its capacities to marshal the will and the imagination toward creative practice. This methodical cultiva-tion of habit falls under a heading of "piety," the practiced ratification of cul-tural memory or, more simply, a commitment to remember tradition through performance.

Of method in prayer—conceived as a *machina memorialis* for producing the socialized subjectivity of habitus—one finds no shortage. There is method in prayer's performative genres and scripts in all modes. These extend from the smallest units of gesture, such as blessing oneself with holy water, making a sign of the cross, bowing at particular words, or facing toward Mecca, to the scripting of elaborate rituals that coordinate the actions of many across multiple modes of performance to embody its conceptually abstract scenes. Extemporaneous or "free" prayer, rooted in models of practice that valorize authenticity and local inspiration, is no less methodical for being oral than textual prayer is, though its methods are less obviously mechanical than prayer's explicit "engines." Extemporaneous prayer also relies on commonplaces to structure what to say to divine beings and how to say it. In all these practices, the connections between memory, method, and prayer appear ever more substantial the more closely one examines prayer. As classical and medieval rhetorical practitioners were keenly aware, memory requires method, whether through the construction of elaborate mental palaces or by other performative means.

In addressing prayer as both an embodied and a cultural practice, rhetoric's historically neglected canon of memory emerges as a fruitful site of inquiry. Beyond simple models of rote memorization and sophisticated models of storage and retrieval, the canon of memory serves to connect cognitive, social, and material dimensions of prayer. Memory is the material—what Carruthers calls the "mental flour"—upon which prayer operates in building character. Reading the tradition-steeped Memorare reveals that prayer is an art of memory on multiple levels. Above all, it is a socialized craft involving agents who comprise a community of practice, drawing on a shared stock of spiritual resources, employing the same spiritual tools, and extending beyond local and immediate contexts of utterance.

That said, our examination of prayer as memory reveals that the canon of memory is inherently diffuse, with different aspects of memory being activated in different rhetorical situations. Functioning so thoroughly as a system of memory, prayer has an invaluable role to play in reconstituting memory as a living canon of rhetoric.

Finally, prayer offers welcome opportunities to discover how long-standing notions of rhetoric's canons may be both productively juxtaposed and integrated into performative wholes. For memory, it becomes clear, interacts with invention (as it does with style and other dimensions of performance). Tracing the manifold character of memory found to be active in the Memorare allows us to see memory as a means by which to chart linkages of all kinds within individual minds and bodies and across communities. Allowing memory to remain flexible and to operate at different scales and in different ways in our accounts of rhetorical action will *enable* memory to be a productive site of inquiry in dynamic relation with other canons and other critical concepts of rhetoric. Prayer emerges as a site of rhetorical practice in which memory's range of operations is more powerfully demonstrated in response to the entire range of symbolic practices by which we constitute ourselves in community with others.

6

BODIES AND SPIRITS IN VIRTUAL MOTION: PRAYER AND DELIVERY IN CYBERSPACE

My words fly up, my thoughts remain below;
Words without thoughts never to heaven go.

—Shakespeare, *Hamlet*

My feet were praying.

—Rabbi Abraham Heschel, on marching with Dr. King

Before the communicative resources of the radio or the Internet were ever imagined, the material character of prayer as "action at a distance" was memorably addressed in a confessional aside by *Hamlet*'s Claudius: "My words fly up, my thoughts remain below; / Words without thoughts never to heaven go" (3.3.97–98). Claudius knows why his prayer has failed: having confessed to the murder of his brother the king, he cannot bring himself to repent. This scene of revelation and misinterpretation—Hamlet mistakenly thinks he is witnessing a contrite Claudius—is typically read as clear evidence of Hamlet's debilitating hesitation. But it can also be read for what it reveals about how we understand prayer's many-sided character as thought, word, and deed.

Claudius discovers that, because he is unwilling to relinquish the fruits of his regicide, he cannot pray authentically and obtain forgiveness. Still, he kneels in knowing and futile desperation, as if to gain absolution without renouncing his illegitimate kingship and marriage. This outward gesture of piety inadvertently deters Hamlet from avenging his father, lest killing Claudius in the act of prayer send him to heaven instead of hell.[1]

Claudius's admission of insincerity employs a commonplace in Christian tradition that, for prayer to be successful, it must be genuine. Outer form must mirror inner intention. Appropriate words and gestures are insufficient. This admission also reflects an established notion that, proper conditions observed, prayer does indeed "travel" from human source to divine destination despite psychic or metaphorical distance between the two. Words "fly up" when they serve as vehicle for proper thoughts.[2] This understanding of words as vehicle is an instance of the "conduit metaphor" for communication analyzed by Michael Reddy. In this metaphor, words are containers for thoughts, feelings, and intentions placed within them. Claudius's prayer fails to reach its destination because his words are empty vessels.

Flying heavenward on sincere words is only one metaphor for what prayer does, albeit a common one; others include opening a communicative space between pray-ers and prayed-to. And, in Saint John Damascene's classic formulation, prayer is a "raising of one's mind and heart to God" (qtd. in Martin 113), where it brings not merely words or thoughts but the whole person—epitomized by reason and passion—into the presence of the divine. The notion of prayer as a means of transport underscores the extent to which discourse with the divine is understood as transcending space. In strictly physical terms, no travel takes place. The movement of prayer, as opposed to the gestures of those who pray, is psychic or metaphorical.

This brief examination of a scene of apparent prayer points to two fundamental ways of understanding prayer: something takes place; and something goes somewhere—a dialectic of stasis and motion. At any given moment, one of these conceptual frames will be dominant. In emphasizing prayer as situation and motive, the focus of previous chapters has been largely on prayer in static terms. In this final chapter, the focus turns to prayer as movement, whether psychic or metaphorical. Claudius (or Shakespeare) has it right: one's *attitude* in praying is instrumental in whether one's prayer reaches its destination. Equally so, an inward focus on intention must finally be expressed outwardly to facilitate prayer's movement from "here" to "there." These deictics signal that prayer is something en route, a discourse in transit. Prayer sets spirits and bodies in motion to communicate with beings conceived as of another world. To capture both the dynamic character and the goal of prayer, we need to press a key term from the rhetorical tradition into service: *delivery.*

The fifth and last of rhetoric's traditional canons, delivery is concerned with performance. Delivery is rhetoric at its most outward and instrumental. As delivery, prayer actualizes the relationships between its communicative agents. In simplest terms, we begin with the recognition that prayer is not only something said, but also something *sent.* As delivery, prayer assumes outward form as speech or gesture. In these forms, it "travels," entering other rhetorical bodies.

There is here both a literal sense of delivery, in communicating messages, and a figurative one, in being freed of burdens.

This chapter first addresses matters of location and transport in prayer with a focus on the rhetorical canon of delivery, whose contemporary analogue is performance. It then extends notions of prayer as delivery to consider prayer beyond the body in the virtual domains of cyberspace. In particular, it examines practices of online prayer at two sponsored websites to understand how notions of delivery are realized there. I argue that prayer readily "colonizes" cyberspace because it is discourse already and profoundly invested in notions of transport and the virtual.

Indeed, given prayer's remote addressees and its strategies for invoking the real, prayer can be considered the original virtual reality technology. That is to say, prayer is a techné for communicating with the real as it is experienced virtually and mediated materially. Prayer's adaptability across both modes (oral, written, kinetic) and space depends significantly on the inherent virtuality in all its communicative performance. References here to the "virtual" are meant to suggest an intersection between the domains of religion and technology whose importance has yet to be fully recognized. Religion is generally imagined in cognitive rather than material terms. But books, statuary, candles, and incense are just some of the many material objects that serve as tools to assist practitioners in attaining and maintaining a proper frame of mind and in engaging in imaginative acts of worship and spiritual communion.[3]

As we think about the use of tangible objects to connect with the intangible, let us consider the religious and technological senses of *icon*. In religious terms, an *icon* (or image), a polychrome representation of a holy figure, is an aid to devotion, whereas an *idol* is an object *of* devotion. In *God Without Being* and other works, philosopher Jean-Luc Marion limns the phenomenological distinction between *icon* and *idol*. Marion argues for a "showing forth" of the invisible reality of the icon behind its visible one. Whereas the icon is never a reduction of the invisible to the visible, the idol is precisely that: its visible reality is *all* there is to it.[4]

Although Marion addresses the false worship of idols in theological concepts more than in actual worship practices, it is highly significant that he centers his concern in the modality of vision and in the religious icon, whose pictorial "gaze" meets the beholder: "The icon properly manifests the nuptial distance that weds, without confusing, the visible and the invisible—that is, the human and the divine. The idol tries to abolish that distance through the availability of the god who is placed permanently within the fixity of a face" (*Idol and Distance* 9). Maintaining while at the same time overcoming distance is central to the rhetoric of prayer as an encounter of the real through the virtual.

The religious sense of *icon* can be compared with its technological sense. A computer icon serves as a manipulable representation in the visual field of the graphical user interface, something users interact with to perform vital operations such as opening and closing file folders on a virtual desktop. As different as these senses of *icon* appear, in effect, a single notion is at work here. In each case, an icon visually represents something inaccessible except through virtual contact. And in each case, the icon functions as means of interaction with virtual objects or beings. The notions of iconicity and virtuality will prove to be of service in developing notions of prayer as mediated performance concerned with the potential of various modes to access and represent the real.

Prayer and Modes of Delivery

To begin, some questions: *Where* is prayer? When prayers are sent, where do they *go*? Tilting in different directions, these questions suggest a dialectic of stasis and movement in prayer. On the one hand, prayer's whereabouts can be imagined in terms of location. Prayer is an activity associated with dedicated sites such as churches, temples, mosques, and other sacred locales. In figurative terms, prayer is associated with interior locations such as the heart or mind. On the other hand, prayer can be understood as motion, as translation in space. To the extent that divine beings are understood to be "out there," prayer is conceived as an effort to "get there."

In "Here, There, and Anywhere," anthropologist Jonathan Z. Smith classifies religions of classical and late antiquity in specifically deictic terms: "(1) The 'here' of domestic religion, located primarily in the home and in burial sites; (2) the 'there' of public, civic, and state religions, largely based in temple constructions; and (3) the 'anywhere' of a rich diversity of religious formations that occupy an interstitial space between these other two loci" (23). This taxonomy recognizes location, but also dislocation, in ritual activity associated with specific sites in the social landscape of religion. Potential for dislocation becomes ever more pronounced in the religions of late antiquity, a development Smith characterizes as a shift from spatial notions of "place" to temporal notions of "taking place," with corresponding migration of ritual activity from "here" and "there" to "any-where." Our understanding of prayer is shaped by these deictic notions, which, variously, sacralize local environments, orchestrate movement toward dedicated sites of worship, and authorize forms of worship that may take place virtually anywhere. Each of these conceptions of where human and divine beings come into contact differently configures a scene of prayer as a complex of location and performance. Whether prayer calls down divine beings or elevates human beings; whether human beings travel to where the divine is found or their prayers do so, prayer manifests some element of translation through space.

Complexities of prayer and place have been richly examined by sociologist Robert Orsi, whose *Thank You, St. Jude* and other works investigate devotional shrines in the United States. In "The Center Out There, In Here, and Everywhere Else," Orsi notes that the Baltimore-based National Shrine to Saint Jude, patron saint of hopeless causes, eventually developed an adjunct devotional practice for those who could not travel to the shrine in person. They could, instead, write and mail in prayers of petition and thanksgiving. Orsi calls this form of partici-pation "writing as going" (212). Most interesting about "writing as going" is that the technology of writing had already become a standard practice at the physical shrine before its keepers afforded petitioners a virtual pilgrimage, with many visi-tors depositing their written petitions there. Under appropriate circumstances, written messages substitute for speech and for one's physical presence. In lieu of visiting, a letter is a token of presence when communicating at a distance. These affordances of text in combination with the technology of a postal system in which mail is rapidly collected and distributed allow for a virtual pilgrimage to, but also real participation at, physical sites of devotion. (The parallel here to prayer in cyberspace will become evident later in the chapter.)

The affordances of "writing as going" parallel those of "speaking as going" at the heart of prayer. Of course, someone might simply have chosen to pray to Saint Jude directly without the need for a pilgrimage, real or virtual, to a physical shrine. Neither travel nor text was necessary. Nevertheless, the physical shrine maintains its status as a devotional site even as other options for prayer are possible. Orsi's findings reveal prayer's complexities as a rhetoric of delivery. Prayer's conceptual scenes of address must be manifested in actual performance, in which the affordances and constraints of various modes are essential ele-ments of the rhetorical act, chiefly at the motivational level of *agency* or, more precisely, the *agency-act* relation. In classical rhetoric, this relation ("ratio") is apprehended under the heading of "delivery."

Delivery (Latin *actio*; Greek *hypokrisis*) is concerned with the means of expression, with the realization of discourse in performance, and with affordances of mode. Like memory, rhetoric's fourth canon, delivery has been neglected in favor of rhetoric's "major" canons: invention, arrangement, and style. This neglect may be attributed largely to the rise of text as a medium of communication. Delivery is the rhetorical canon most rooted, seemingly, in oral modes of performance, as reflected in its historical association with matters of vocal pronouncement (*pronuntiatio*) and gesture (*actio*).[5] In the transition from oral to written modes, from embodied speech to disembodied text, delivery effectively became lost in translation. The electric media of telephone, radio, and television, however, ushered in a communications revolution, one that returned delivery to prominence and that Walter Ong has identified as "secondary orality" in his book *Orality and Literacy* (11). Subsequent developments in technology giving rise to digital media have extended delivery's lease. Delivery's traditional association with speech has become less clear. Delivery may be seen, now, to encompass a broader range of concerns, including social relations between agents in a mediated rhetorical exchange.

This approach to delivery places prayer at a nexus of two distinct frames: the *dramatic* and the *transactional*. In dramatic terms, prayer's speakers and audiences may be imagined as active agents and passive recipients, for example. In transactional terms, speakers and audiences are implicated in complementary relations based on what takes place in prayer (information exchanged, obligations recognized, promises made or fulfilled). In terms of speech-act theory, this is a distinction between illocutionary (dramatic) and perlocutionary (transactional) dimensions of utterance. Delivery realizes both dramatic and transactional relations between discursive agents. More pointedly, we can speak of delivery as the "interface" in a mediated encounter. More lyrically, we can speak of the element of mystery by which discourse across modes acts with force, even at a distance, upon agents.

The choice of "interface" suggests parallels between face-to-face communication in oral performance and the virtual points of contact between users and technology in computer-mediated communication. The point to be emphasized is that the canon of delivery spans modes of performance precisely because what is delivered transcends its medium, even as it cannot take place without a medium. This insight is implicit in classical rhetoric's understanding of delivery as a multimodal performance experienced as embodied practice. Thus, in oral contexts, it is impossible to conceive of communication as anything less than bimodal. Where chapters 4 and 5 considered the role of the body in approaching prayer as attitude and as memory, the present chapter sees the body as located in a social landscape that mediates rhetorical performance.

The rhetoric of delivery is made especially striking in a celebrated contrast between two ways of performing prayer: "And when you pray, you shall not be like the hypocrites. For they love to pray standing in the synagogues and on the corners of the streets, that they may be seen by men. Assuredly, I say to you, they have their reward. But you, when you pray, go into your room, and when you have shut your door, pray to your Father who is in the secret place; and your Father who sees in secret will reward you openly" (Matt. 6:5–6, NKJV). This passage from the Sermon on the Mount features Jesus's criticism of hypocritical (literally "playacting") prayer. Jesus likens this manner of prayer to Greek dramatic performance, where the hypocrite is a stage actor, complete with mask that conceals the actor's true identity even as it amplifies his speech and exaggerates his features for his human audience. Ostentatious in prayer before others, the hypocrite receives his immediate reward.

In contrast to this playacting, what Jesus proposes amounts to "*pray*acting." Contrasted here are distinct scenes of delivery situated in differently imagined contexts with different audiences, purposes—and outcomes. Jesus would have his followers avoid praying openly as a mere theatrical act but instead pray in secret, in direct communion with God, who will reward them openly.

Of course, retreat to the privacy of one's prayer room is no guarantee that the prayer offered there will succeed, as shown by Claudius's failure. Nor is the matter of where to pray in relation to where that prayer *goes* settled by such normative pronouncements. Both synagogue and street corner remain places where prayer is addressed to both human and divine audiences. Today, the street corner may be a public forum on the Internet, and the synagogue, a virtual prayer room online. That said, let us now examine mediated spaces in which prayer is separated from the body of its performer in the virtual domains of cyberspace.

Delivering Prayer in a Digital Age

The development of digital modes of communication presents opportunities to observe the extent to which emerging practices "remediate" existing ones. *Remediation*, or "the representation of one medium in another," is a term introduced by media theorists Jay David Bolter and Richard Grusin to account for the process by which one medium imitates, borrows from, and reshapes another (45). Thus text remediates speech, as film does text. This term is especially applied to "new" media, but remediation is arguably as old as human communication itself. Indeed, prayer as song, not simply speech, is among the earliest of our "mediated extensions," to use the term as Marshall McLuhan does in his seminal *Understanding Media*. Long basic to the logic of artistic creation, remediation acquires renewed agency with the enormous capacities of digital networks for access, transmission, and storage.

Religion has been as active as any other domain in going digital. Almost with the advent of digital technology, religion began a migration from face-to-face encounters in dedicated physical sites to virtual encounters between individuals and institutions through e-mail, the World Wide Web, and other forms of synchronous and asynchronous digital communication. In this migration, a wide range of emerging practices of religion in the form of cyberchurches and other cyberworship has arisen to remediate existing practices.[6]

To help make sense of developments in digital communication as these bear on religion, Christopher Helland draws a useful distinction between "religion online" and "online religion." *Religion online* refers to an Internet presence for religious material existing outside of digital networks, to include websites for bricks-and-mortar churches and online repositories of information about religion. *Online religion*, by contrast, involves the use of digital communication "to create new forms of networked spiritual interactions" (Campbell 7). These new forms include cyberworship and virtual pilgrimages.

Among the most common devotional practices to be found online, prayer/prayer request sites number, conservatively, in the tens of thousands. They invite their visitors to participate in the form of prayers or requests for prayers. Contributors respond with prayers or prayer requests of their own and, in some cases, with responses to those of others. Although, in many ways, such online activity replicates similar activity offline, its replication merits attention for what it reveals about prayer as a cognitive, social, and material practice in the context of delivery.

Noting that a robust examination of cyberprayer in its many variations is beyond the scope of the present work, we can examine two representative sites and get at least a general sense of prayer's remediation in cyberspace. Differences among online prayer websites are far from negligible. Some sites invite only contributions of prayers or prayer requests but do not post them, whereas many others post those contributions, making them available to other site visitors.

Still other sites also allow for threaded, interactive responses to prayers or prayer requests. Some even screen what is posted for appropriate content, require registration to participate, or otherwise establish rules of etiquette for posting. Let us consider, then, two websites (one recent and one current) that illustrate the performance of prayer online conceived as delivery, beginning with a recent prayer request website that, though typical of its genre in several respects, was as sophisticated as it was simple.

The Church of England's website Say ONE for Me (http:/www.sayoneforme. org) was an effort in pastoral outreach created in 2010 by a cluster of dioceses in the Church of England for the express purpose of soliciting prayers or prayer requests from any who might choose to respond during the Lenten season.[7] Except for its seasonal, six-week window—most prayer websites operate indefinitely—Say ONE for Me was hardly exceptional among the many sectarian or church-based websites. Yet this now former website stood out for its functional simplicity. Its home page featured a minimalist white background, a modest amount of text, and a handful of images. The site was designed with one aim: to encourage visitors to contribute their prayers or prayer requests. "Welcome to Say ONE for Me," it read, "a new website from the Church of England that's asking for your prayer." This greeting explained that the site's bishop sponsors would "pray for you" when you "send it," and asked someone who might be skeptical, "What have you got to lose by asking God for what you need?" The text reassured visitors that their prayers would remain anonymous. They needed only to compose them within the text box provided and click "Amen" to deliver them to the bishops.

In an upper band on the site's home page (Lent 2011), together with the site's logo, were images of an elderly, a middle-aged, and a younger woman (who happened to be black), as well as of a middle-aged and a younger man (whose attire suggested he might be a manual or technical worker). All five subjects looked directly into the camera and toward the site's visitors. To the right of these images, a rounded rectangular box framed the text "Say ONE for Me" and featured a pointed outdent suggestive of a speaking voice as the source of the text. This speech balloon graphic was repeated beneath the upper band and opposite the site's primary text, where it encircled a conventional text box labeled "Prayer" suitable for actual composing, with an "Amen" button beneath it for sending the completed prayer.

Despite its visual and verbal simplicity, the site reflected significant assumptions and considered judgments in inviting visitors to compose and deliver their

prayers. It is worth examining how this invitation was offered and what was to
be done with the prayers delivered. First, the site made no reference to requests
for prayer, only to prayer itself. And, second, it neither prompted visitors with
suggestions nor proposed guidelines for them. Thus a visitor was encouraged to
think of any text he or she might enter as a prayer, even if it took the form of a
request for prayer or explanation of a situation for which prayer was appropriate. At the same time, because the site was quite explicit that its bishops "will
pray for you," any text "spoken" into the text box could be thought of as both a
request for prayer and a prayer itself.

And because the site was "asking for your prayer," a visitor was placed in
the position of grantor, not merely petitioner. This invitation was warm and
respectful. For those who chose to accept it, three interlaced acts of petition
would occur: an initiating request by the website "asking for your prayer";
the responses of visitors either as prayers or requests for prayers; and, finally,
the prayers to be performed by the bishops when they took up the visitors'
responses.

The website's title, Say ONE for Me, was studiously casual. It was what you
might tell someone more devout than you as that person headed off to church.
In this vein, the site's title alluded to the 1959 movie *Say One for Me*, starring
Bing Crosby as a parish priest who saved souls among the hard-bitten denizens
of New York's theater world, where he often encountered this mildly irreverent
remark. The site's title offset the irreverent impression of that allusion with a
shift in tone and typography. It read not "Say One for Me" but, rather, "Say
ONE for Me." Just this *one* prayer, the site proposed—a meaningful, yet modest
act entailing no further commitment. Unlike some sites, it did not ask participants to provide either their names or their e-mail addresses.

When a visitor decided to "pray" into the text box, this act became an undi-
luted participation at an individual level in a broader collective act, as well as
a response to an invitation. The website existed in a chain of discourse at once
invitational, interventional, and intercessory. Say ONE for Me invited participation in a belief that prayers are "out there" to be called into discourse. In this
respect, the website was a *sponsoring agent*.[8] This invitation asked for a textual
response, identified as prayer by the sponsors. Say ONE for Me thus functioned
as an intervention reaching out to persons in need. In the context of delivery,
it prompts consideration of how a response to such an invitation is a material
act of prayer and how the invitation and response together unfurl within and
beyond cyberspace. The broadest frame that may be placed around this discourse

is "intercession," discourse linking multiple agents and audiences in a complex chain of performance. But where in this chain does prayer begin and end?

Indeed, where in a response to this website's invitation is prayer to be found? Locating prayer in a chain of interlaced acts is revelatory of prayer as delivery. One answer lies in a distinction between "prayer" as an accomplished act and "praying" as an ongoing activity. We can locate praying in the activity of composing—a process rather than a product. Praying takes place on the visitor's side in this asynchronous digital exchange. It involves the mental spaces employed in composing and delivering a prayer by clicking "Amen." A second, corresponding instance of praying occurs when the recipient of this delivered text performs a similar activity on behalf of the sender, taking up that prayer and reperforming it.

Yet Say One for Me and similar sites suggest that the rhetorical action of prayer is more diffuse, its location less determinate, and its performative arc more extensive than what is implied by the scenario of praying at one node of a network to be followed by praying at another. A different parsing of this communicative event is possible. Consider that prayer begins before discourse and ends only when, having been delivered, it is also *received*. In chapter 2, the reciprocal relations of delivery and reception were characterized in terms of "address" and "being heard." In immediate contexts, delivery and reception are considered to be simultaneous even if this is not always the case. Rhetorical affect—the response of an audience to discourse—can be drawn out or delayed, just as delivery can.[9]

In online prayer, the conceptual immediacy of delivery and reception is complicated by distance, hence the distinction between prayer as said and as *sent*. The act of composing (or saying) a prayer and the corresponding, but conceptually or materially distinct, act of sending it to other nodes in a linked network of websites (where others may access, read, print, and add their "Amen" to it) allow for praying participants to experience both the immediacy of praying and the distributed unfurling of prayer in a scene of reception. What is important in this scene is that human audiences serve both as recipients and as relayers of discourse destined, ultimately, for a divine audience. In this scene, individual acts of praying cohere into an intricately textured mosaic of discursive activity, an activity that involves praying for and with others, beside praying to God.

In cyberspace, prayer depends as much on the remediation of gesture as of voice. In Say One for Me, voice is remediated as text and as gesture in clicking "Amen"—both the verbal ending and material *sending* of a prayer. Thus is the intention—"amen" means "so be it"—to deliver a prayer rendered materially in language and, finally, bodily action. Indeed, in the performative logic of online delivery systems, mental operations can only be manifested through the actions of fingers interacting tactilely with a screen or keyboard. The computer keyboard, terminal, and other elements of wired and, increasingly, wireless networks are extensions of our physical body as an interactive instrument for social performance.

The distributed delivery of intercessory prayer is particularly responsive to the affordances of digital networks. As both stationary websites and traveling messages, this technological infrastructure actualizes a delivery system that anticipates and enacts social as well as digital networks. These relationships link multiple addressees (and digital addresses) as acts that witness to prayer's rhetorical power. Prayer's migration into digital networks is encouraged by a corresponding delivery system, one in which prayer's conceptual architecture is mirrored in virtual networks. Delivering a prayer by typing a message and clicking "Amen" is thus but a partial act. Delivery must be understood within a social and material network of relations. Delivery is consummated only when its rhetorical force combines with the acts of others in a network of invitation, transmission, and reception.

The sequence of invitation, response, reception, and affirmation—of prayer and prayer again—manifested in Say ONE for Me is a translation into digital communication of activity that occurs offline. Prayer is routinely invited and welcomed by religious persons and communities. A prayer/prayer request website remediates these offline practices to expand the circle of those who may be brought into a network of prayer. In online prayer, one need not be in the physical presence of, or in social intimacy with, those with whom one interacts. Online sites thus remediate immediate and interpersonal communication with broader reach and the option of anonymity. In this respect, online sites remediate practices enacted through both speech and writing in nondigital settings. One may worship at online prayer shrines much as one participates in votive activities by mailing a prayerful text to the National Shrine of Saint Jude or by physically placing a written prayer at a material shrine. Indeed, online remediation of offline practices and locations blurs the boundary between the real and the virtual. The physically located shrine of Saint Jude is no less a virtual space of communion with the divine for being manifested in the material than an online shrine one can visit to perform similar acts of petition or thanksgiving.

A Benedictine monastery physically located in Cullman, Alabama, Saint Bernard's Abbey offers an illuminating case of remediation in the context of devotion. At the chapel's website, St Bernard Abbey's Online Chapel (http:// ubiamor.org), a visitor is encouraged to pray and, correspondingly, to light a virtual candle as an automated effect of composing his or her prayer in the text box provided. Each of a handful of chapels at a visitor's disposal features a similar array of votive niches, typically fifteen in number, into which icons of virtual candles have been placed. An animated graphic of a "flickering" candle indicates that a previous beseecher has "left" a prayer in that niche. The candle's height indicates how near it is to being extinguished. In some chapels, candles remain lit for a week, in others for two weeks. Visitors to this virtual abbey must find available candles on which to place their prayers. Yet, unlike a visitor to a real chapel, a visitor to the online chapel is free to click on any lit candle and read prayers left by others through the affordances of text and digital storage.

Most visitors to the online chapel will find this remediated practice intuitive, especially if they are familiar with actual chapels. Despite efforts to re-create an actual devotional space online, however, differences remain between the virtual chapel and its physical counterpart. Online, no monetary offering is expected to cover replacement costs for the candle. (In an odd twist, the online prayer chapel is an undertaking of the monastery's real-world candle shop.) Even so, candles "burn out," as they would in an actual setting, so that others may make use of the space. What is more significant, sensory experiences of sight, sound, and smell are lacking in the virtual chapel. Only some suggestive iconography of saints, a stone-like background, and the icons of the candles themselves offer visual cues that allow visitors to imagine they have entered a chapel.

The most substantial difference between prayer in the virtual chapel and in the physical one involves translating the act of prayer from speech to text. In the online chapel, one leaves a textual trace of one's prayer in addition to a "lit" candle; this makes prayer a public, if anonymous, act. In a physical chapel, one's prayer can remain unspoken. Of course, being physically present in the chapel is itself a public act. That any visitor can view the prayers and intentions left by others within various niches gives this act a very different character from what occurs in an actual chapel. By comparison with Say ONE for Me, this online chapel offers a small text window to establish expectations that prayerful intentions should be brief. The parallel asynchronous acts at the chapel—first one visitor, then another—are not explicitly intercessory; no one promises these prayers will be taken up in prayer by others. That said, the visibility of multiple prayers together in a virtual space contributes to the experience of participation in a communal act. Each candle burns not only for its individual intention but in sympathy with others.

In both actual and virtual settings, a lit candle is a material trace marking the delivery of a devotional act, one initiated in desire and transformed into articulate thought. Lighting a candle, whether actually or virtually, is a corresponding gesture of delivery with the performance of speech, whether voiced or silent, actual or virtual. The candle itself is a mediated extension of the body as a site of rhetorical delivery. In material form, it symbolizes and prolongs the immaterial act of prayer to give it physical or visible presence and duration. Indeed, a lighted candle extends in time and locates in space delivery of a prayer "sent" to an addressee insofar as the candle continues to pray on behalf of its sponsor.

These two prayer websites are virtual to the extent that the forms and practices they reproduce are digital derivations of their offline counterparts. In some sense, a communication face to face seems more "real" than one based in virtual encounters. At least, physical sites may be deemed qualitatively different from their online counterparts in that their material manifestation "counts" as a greater investment in the real. A votive shrine or intercessory prayer circle, online or offline, is a complex activity system, one that involves multiple agents cooperatively engaged in interlocking rhetorical acts of delivery. I characterize online modes of prayer in terms similar to offline modes insofar as they mediate (or remediate) relationships experienced as connection and presence. In social terms, online sites, like their offline counterparts, provide for the performance of discourse in a prayerful context of community, solidarity, and witness. Rather than offer something radically new, what online prayer websites do is actualize the logic already implicit in prayer as a virtual site of delivery.

This logic, I have suggested, resides in conceptions of rhetorical performance as delivery with its counterpart in reception. As utterance, prayer is incomplete until it has been heard. As performance, prayer remains undelivered until it has been received. And unless it is delivered by some means, prayer remains unrealized as discourse. There are social motives for frustrating efficient delivery, for prayer too easily delivered is insufficiently reverent discourse.

Intercessory prayer reaches its destination by a circuitous route, through human or divine intermediaries who amplify and corroborate a prayer. Through their assistance, communication with remote and intangible beings is experienced more concretely. Indeed, all of prayer's delivery strategies function to make the virtual real through technology. Prayer is grounded, insistently so, in the materiality of bodies and language and their mediated extensions. As an inherently virtual scene of communication, prayer materializes the immaterial. Consequently, there is nothing really new in prayer's migration to cyberspace, including the use of digital tools to "text" God. Long ago, prayer anticipated cyberspace as a medium for virtual communication.

Though I stress continuity between cyberspace and other settings, online interaction differs significantly from its face-to-face counterpart. Online, one can be both "here" and "there." Echoing Jonathan Z. Smith, one may be virtually *anywhere* online. Yet too much can be made of the spiritual resources of cyberspace. The Internet does not perfect the delivery of prayer. It affords opportunities for communion through its configurations of presence. These configurations can be said to "disappear" when a medium is experienced in immediate terms. Prayer negotiates a vital divide between immediacy and *hyper*mediacy. As Jay Bolter and Richard Grusin characterize this "double logic of mediation," in immediacy, the medium of delivery or reception effectively retreats from view, whereas in hypermediacy, the perception of mediation is reinforced (2).

Prayer is ever at risk of collapsing into immediacy and, thus, losing its meta-rhetorical character as a virtual act. In drawing attention to the medium, prayer resembles "pure persuasion," characterized by Burke in *A Rhetoric of Motives* as a "grim kind of coyness" or "standoffishness" essential to perpetuating some division in the social order (270–71). Pointing to the artifice necessary to maintain a dramatic performance, Burke cites actors' relations to audiences as "perhaps as near an instance of 'pure persuasion' as one can find" (270). Reading prayer as a rhetoric of delivery emphasizes both its material dimension as a necessary instrument for communication and its social dimension as a mode of "self-interference" required to maintain the distance as well as the "courtship" to which prayer is committed (270–71).

As a rhetoric of delivery, prayer represents embodied performance in terms of destinations, locations, and modes of transmission. Beyond these concerns, a final locale must be considered in prayer's origin. Indeed, if we imagine delivery as extending in time both forward and backward from a performance, we might inquire not where prayer goes but where prayer *has been*. In the situational terms with which this inquiry began in chapter 1, prayer is discourse that emerges from and in response to conditions of need and opportunity. In terms of delivery, prayer's origin can be identified as a matter of transport. Prayer comes from and is addressed to agents, not only situations. It is a response to an other, even as it is addressed to some other. As I have argued throughout, prayer's character remains fundamentally ethical in being *called for*, not simply by exigent circumstances, but by others, human and divine. Its character as address is as much a response to an invocation as it is an invocation itself.

The invitation to pray both for and with others precedes any active response. As evident in the websites examined here, prayer is *sponsored* discourse. Invited prayer is called forth by individuals and institutions, by beings human and divine. Prayer is also shared with others in acts of witness and co-creation. These acts may be actual or, as Jesus cautions, hypocritical, as a form of playacting. As hypocrisy, these acts do not speak adequately or accurately to their situation; rather, they are performed as apostrophic address that extends no further than its immediate scene; they are performed for show. In contrast, real prayer exists within an encompassing scene of discourse, a scene that extends in time and space beyond its local occasion of utterance and that is experienced as a dialogic response to situations—a form of acting, but also of being acted upon.

Before prayer is uttered, it is discourse already in transit—a form of spiritual transport. As such, prayer's work is to extend bodies and spirits through virtual motion. Finally, then, prayer can be understood as the dynamic principle implicit in discourse, coursing as the lifeblood through the communities it constitutes.

CONCLUSION
DOES RHETORIC HAVE A PRAYER?

In the twenty-first century, the prayer room Jesus commends to his followers in his Sermon on the Mount (Matt. 6:5–6), a space to which one may retreat in all humility, often comes with a laptop or mobile device and 24/7 connectivity. The proverbial street corner where one's piety may be put on display is now more likely to involve a digital posting to a social network site. The latest technologies blur the division between private and public on which Jesus's admonition depends. Increasingly, religious expression is performed using the same tools we check the weather or read our e-mail with. Increasingly, we place much of our life on some sort of public display. Indeed, unless we retreat to the desert, at least figuratively, it becomes increasingly difficult to be out of digital range.

If there is a lesson in this era of "always on," it is in the communicative potential of technology. This lesson, I believe, is the lesson of prayer, understood as the perfection of the possibility of connection and the promise of response, epitomized in commercials that celebrate the promise of full signal strength everywhere: "Can you hear me now?" Yet, in other ways, the paradigm of "always on" challenges fundamental assumptions on which prayer depends as an art of discourse, principally, its capacity to overcome estrangement and to structure the momentous. Prayer's phenomenological and rhetorical texture crucially depends on the possibilities of entering an alternative space in which beings of radically different orders can genuinely communicate. In a culture that relishes self-exposure, voiced prayer presents one of the few remaining opportunities for embarrassment, not only from being overheard but even more so from overhearing others pray. Private prayer performed in public puts witnesses in a position of discomfort, as when we hear others in intimate conversation on their cell phones.

No doubt digital technology will continue to have a profound effect on the practices of prayer. At the same time, the laments or shout-outs that currently circulate throughout social networks are not so different from the protest and praise of Scripture. This is not simply because biblical texts supply models for

religious oratory even now, but because prayer's concerns and discursive operations are as universal in scope as they are diverse in form. Just as writing radically transformed the way we practice religion, so will digital media, yet prayer
remains a fundamentally conservative manifestation of our social condition as
languaged beings.

In charting various courses across the territory of prayer, I have tried my best to
remember the wise adage that the map is not the territory. I set out equipped with
the critical tools of rhetoric, but also with the hope that these tools would not
overdetermine my encounter with prayer. If anything, I realized, the task was as
much to meet prayer through rhetoric as it was to meet rhetoric through prayer—
to see the specific in the general and the general in the specific—and, for good
measure, the familiar in the strange and the strange in the familiar. The metaphor
of the rediscovered country underscores that the task is one of seeing anew something that has been there all along, something that, for one reason or another, we
have lost the ability or the interest to see. I proposed that seeing prayer is quite a
challenging task: the things that make prayer prayer are parts of the discourse that
lies at the very core of our nature as beings who communicate through symbolic
language. Consequently, it is not the surface features of prayer—those which set
prayer apart from other discourse and even make it strange—that are most interesting and significant, but the features that *align* prayer with other discourse.

In closing, I pause to consider whether and to what extent prayer figures
in rhetoric's future. It is clear to me that prayer has much to offer in trimming
rhetoric's sails, to employ yet another metaphor. Attention to prayer has the
potential to reinvigorate many of rhetoric's key concepts and to raise important
questions about what we are doing both when we practice rhetoric and when
we simply profess it. As I claimed at the outset, rhetoric's inattention to prayer
in the contemporary era comes as a surprise, if only because so many other subjects now fall within its purview. This inattention itself raises questions. What
is it about prayer that eludes a critical eye? What may be hiding in plain sight?

My response throughout (but especially in chapter 1) has been that prayer can
be understood both as a particular kind of discourse with its range of performative genres and as a particular perspective on discourse—a perspective, I have
argued, that discerns needs and opportunities for discourse. In other words, I
have identified in prayer—or, rather, *as* prayer—rhetoric's situat*ing* (as opposed
to situated) capacities. Indeed, I have looked at prayer as a heuristic art of situation, of mindful attention to the possibilities of ethical discourse. Insofar as
prayer can be distinguished from rhetoric, it is concerned with the purpose of

discourse in relating to others—with beings like ourselves and with beings both like and unlike ourselves. In its essence, prayer positions discourse in a scheme of ethical orientation. In other words, we discover our character through discourse.

I have claimed that prayer's conceptual architecture is as much spatial as it is situational and identified prayer as a space of "rehearsal for living." That is to say, prayer is a site of performance where rhetorical skills are tested in preparation for their tasks in engaging others—the active (speaking) and receptive (listening) dimensions of discourse being of equal concern in prayer. Crucial to sounding prayer's situational depths is the development of an appropriately robust lexicon for engaging the phenomena of prayer, particularly when one considers how steeped in religious terminology the language of prayer is. At the same time, engagement with prayer reveals a surprising resonance with many of rhetoric's key concepts, including kairos and krisis, situation and motive.

What, then, remains to be said of prayer's situations? The account I have presented here seeks to situate prayer in a discursive as well as motivational landscape. The next step is to further sound prayer's depths across the range of its performative occasions. As I have tried to show with my own readings of Reinhold Niebuhr's "Serenity Prayer" and Kenneth Burke's "Dialectician's Hymn," we need more and better readings of prayer as a mode of discourse and of specific prayers as an agency of identity and transformation. We need to better understand how prayer does what it does. And we also need to understand what it does.

The critical method I have employed to discern prayer's multiple dimensions of discourse exploits the utility of Burke's motivational grammar. Discourse at its most motivational, prayer practically calls out to be read through the various prisms defined by this grammar. Prayer as purpose and prayer as agency spring to mind as the most obvious motivational lenses through which to view prayer conceived as a whole. Although it is not unusual to apply Burke's motivational grammar to particular texts, it is far from common to read an entire mode of discourse dramatistically. The approach I have taken does so, but with some distinct departures. I have sought to define prayer operationally through the resources of Burke's grammar by pairing a particular motive with particular rhetorical effects. This is in some sense a modification of Burke's principles of dramatistic relations ("ratios"), hence the three core framings of prayer I have offered: a scene of address, an act of invocation, and an attitude of reverence. Rather than catalog prayer's scenes, acts, or attitudes, I have identified characteristic elements of prayer with the motivational terms of *scene*, *act*, and *attitude*.

My critical readings largely understand prayer through the dimensions of the cognitive (scene of address), the material (act of invocation), and the social (attitude of reverence). All these dimensions are active and mutually implicating at the same time. A scene of address implies an act of invocation implies an attitude of reverence, even as each can be the basis of a discrete reading. Going forward, however, I would propose that other scenes and other acts merit being both singled out and brought together in a more comprehensive account. That said, the reading I have offered is one that seeks to respond to established concerns in rhetorical studies in the belief that rhetoric has an invaluable role to play in speaking to the language of prayer in its particular idiom.

For one such concern, a rhetoric of prayer, in grounding discourse addressed to the divine in notions of linguistic consubstantiality, offers a robust challenge to antirhetorics of prayer (and of discourse broadly) that would ignore rhetorical address as the foundation of social constitutions. A rhetoric of prayer insists on the principle that what enables human and divine communication are precisely those elements which define our human rhetorical potential. This is not an academic question but, rather, a profoundly ethical one. I have suggested that prayer is the site where the range and character of our rhetorical reach are worked out in principle, through practice. In considering prayer as a phenomenon of address, what emerges as most crucial is the dialectic of *address* and *hearing*: prayer is preeminently concerned with the performative conditions for being heard, with what makes for a good prayer. In this respect, prayer represents the most fully developed site of the auditory imagination conceived as our potential to address and to be addressed. Going further, how the range of audiences responsive to rhetorical appeal is conceived, both in theory and in practice, remains a vital concern in rhetoric studies.

One benefit of a dramatistic approach to prayer is the fresh insights that arise from a calculated shift in perspective. In this case, a reversal of priorities from a scene-act to an act-scene relation is a shift from prayer as potential to prayer as kinetic energy. In simplest terms, prayer *does things*. Here, again, rather than catalog the many things prayer can do, its many functions, I have located in prayer an essential function of discourse to call situations into being through the force of utterance, specifically in the speech act of invocation. Hence I have turned (in chapter 3) to strategies for invocation and the anxieties that attend their performance. One might for reasons that are just as compelling turn to strategies of supplication or confession in prayer as invocation for an entirely different reading of prayer's rhetorical moves, as I have illustrated (in chapter

4) in reading prayer as a rhetoric of praise. Any of these actual or imagined readings of prayer in its verbal and other modes merits further development with an emphasis on prayer as a performative rhetoric. My focus on invocation as a site of performance recognizes its distinct character and significance in a rhetoric of prayer, given that invocations call into presence some absent other. Indeed, invocations, with their corresponding vocations, manifest prayer as a transformative agency in articulate acts with real-world consequences: at some level, the gods do come when they are summoned. Invocation is prayer at its most rhetorically dangerous.

A particular danger of invocation arises from conflating invocation (of the real) with apostrophe (to the fictive), a danger ever present. I have highlighted the high stakes of invocation with a brief account of debates among contemporary philosophers (Levinas, Derrida, and Marion) on the nature of the vocative of divine address and predication and on efforts to name the divine in favorable terms. Indeed, the relationship between philosophical, especially phenomenological, accounts of prayer's possibility and purpose and rhetorical approaches to prayer's speech acts (Burke, Bakhtin) remains a promising site for dialogue.

I have contended that prayer is grounded, above all, in the capacity for reverence, conceived in dramatistic terms as a manifestation and performance of attitude and (in chapter 4) that *reverence*, with notions of address and action, is the most accurate available term for prayer's attitude, bringing together the cognitive, material, and social dimensions of prayerful performance. More than affective states such as awe or desire, reverence signals the psychosomatic character of prayer—at once the work of the body and the expression of the soul. Reverence springs from apprehension, acceptance, and articulation of a state of fundamental dependence on beings conceived as both otherworldly and vital to one's very self. With the "Prayer to the Sockeye Salmon" of Kwakiutl culture, which reveals reverence to be articulate expression and embodied practice oriented to right living, I have demonstrated the range of *reverence* as a term straddling the current secular-religious divide. A future focus for rhetoric is to locate and interrogate scenes of reverence in religious and secular guise and to advance a broader understanding of the place of reverence in human and divine affairs.

Burke's treatment of attitude, particularly with respect to secular prayer and piety, reflects the central role of attitude in prayer and of prayer as attitude in the operations of discourse. Indeed, *prayer* emerges as the term closest to *rhetoric* for expressing the operations of mystery and hierarchy seemingly woven into the fabric of communication. The implication of such associations is clear.

Something akin to prayer is here to stay in rhetoric's future as a practical art, whatever the fate of divine beings as presently conceived. The question for the near term remains: What is prayer's place as a subject of critical inquiry under a heading of "rhetoric"?

Divisions in my study suggest distinct lines of future development. On the one hand is a critical rhetoric centered in modern, above all Burkean, approaches. Given the importance of religious concepts to Burke's critical interventions into cognition and culture, not the least of which is his groundbreaking *Rhetoric of Religion*, it is surprising that Burke is not more frequently turned to regarding the discourses of prayer and devotion, from which many of his most potent concepts originate. Yet, as I have endeavored to show, prayer is best approached not through the application of a single method or critical theory, but through a productive pluralism drawing on multiple methodologies and disciplines in concert. The rhetoric of prayer is most robust when it is in dialogue with other accounts of prayer as language and as religion.

On the other hand, multiple strands in rhetorical tradition prove surprisingly responsive to prayer when the focus is on performance and materiality. Accounts of prayer centered in the classical canons of rhetoric suggest that they are presently undervalued sites for critical inquiry, as I have noted (in chapters 5 and 6). My study points in promising directions that link prayer with memory and with delivery, both of which are grounded in the material and bodily dimensions of discourse. A rhetoric of prayer must account for the practices by which discourse is produced and circulated in social networks extensive in time and space.

I have identified prayer (in chapter 5) as a socialized craft of memory, understood as material shared, recollected, and transmitted by individuals and communities in multiple modes and media. Although memory may be regarded as coterminous with thought, with a close reading of the Memorare of Catholic tradition, I have emphasized that memory is rhetorical performance. My treatment of prayer as memory underscores just how much practices of prayer intersect with practices of memory. Anchoring prayer in memory highlights the materiality of discourse, in that communicative tools, including language, are investments in memory. When prayer is recognized as a rhetorical art of memory, its mediated and mediating character comes to the fore as the words, images, texts, gestures, and other memorial modalities structuring the act of communication. Indeed, the most promising avenues for the study of prayer lie at the intersection of rhetoric and media studies. This is particularly so where

prayer is recognized as a site of rhetorical education. Learning to pray is arguably the most widespread formal rhetorical practice, and such learning is intimately bound with practices of memory.

I have claimed (in chapter 6) that the performance of prayer online in dedicated websites raises important questions about the role of communication
technology in the spiritual arts and about delivery more generally. Attention
to prayer as delivery, including digital delivery, signals that what is arguably
the oldest of rhetorical practices is at home with the newest of technologies.
Far from being a historical artifact, prayer shows every sign of maintaining its
vitality in a digital age. It will do so, as it has done in the past, through a range
of spiritual modalities, which must be understood in concert. Prayer is at once
private and public, inward and outward, a performance of speech and gesture. It
is our rhetorical potential for persuasion (including self-persuasion) and identification by appealing to perfect (divine) audiences as manifestations of the real.

So, does rhetoric have a prayer? I believe it does, and hope my efforts to place
prayer and rhetoric into provocative relation will inspire some to set the record
straight and others to explore new avenues of inquiry. Such avenues should
broaden the range of practices considered here to include modes of spiritual
performance outside those of prayer as defined in Western religious practice.
New avenues of inquiry will, I hope, include greater attention to prayer as discourse whose intended rhetorical effects concern human beings at the multiple
levels of clan, community, city, and country, even as it is performed in the direction of divine beings.

By design, I have focused my study on formal operations of prayerful discourse, but implicitly called for extension of these concerns into the realm of
the political as a domain where prayer is used to sanctify, shock, legitimate,
or elevate. Prayer, in its many guises and disguises is a significant domain of
human experience. It manifests a powerful complex of motives driving human
action. The rhetorical danger of our time, perhaps of every time, is twofold:
on the one hand, to make too little of prayer, to discount its value as a site of
character formation; and, on the other, to make too much of prayer by way of
nostalgia for pieties that no longer address our actual situations.

Can recycling be prayer (as I asked in chapter 4)? For that matter, can clean-
ing up streams, demonstrating for peace, agitating for social reform, or tutoring
students in underserved communities? Might these social practices be considered prayerful acts when performed with reverence and in witness to some
higher principle? In this sense, can prayer be any kind of joyful, purposeful

labor? The Benedictine motto of "Pray and work" imagines life as a dynamic engine in which the alternative space of retreat and rehearsal that is prayer gives value to the ordinary sphere of human activity.

For many, work and prayer are experienced as necessary complements for advancing the work of prayer. For some, prayer is where ethical subjectivity may be practiced, social bonds strengthened, and perduring principles realized in dramatic fashion through inclusion of another, ultimate order of being and purpose. Sitting atop, outside, or within the human order, this divine order resituates human affairs in a broader cosmology of meaning and purpose. Within this cosmology, communion between different orders of existence is possible, and thus all forms of rhetorical engagement, identification, and persuasion are also possible. To the extent that practices of remediation are experienced as critical and kairotic work that one is called to do from a sense of obligation and responsibility, prayer will arise as a strategy for encompassing both the reality of that call and the rhetorical agency of response.

Notes

INTRODUCTION

1. Pernot's 2005 plenary address, "The Rhetoric of Religion," was published in *Rhetorica* 24.3 (2006): 235–54. See http://crab.rutgers.edu/~wfitz/pernot.pdf. The 2007 biennial meeting of ISHR, held in Strasbourg, France, was thematically devoted to the intersection of rhetoric and religion.

2. In rhetorical scholarship addressing theology, one can cite Cunningham as well as Webb, *Blessed Excess*; in homiletics, Mountford; and in public discourse, Crowley.

CHAPTER 1

1. In classical mythology, Kairos is represented as a swift-moving figure with a long forelock but otherwise bald to symbolize that fleeting opportunity must be seized before it passes.

2. Richard J. Foster identifies twenty-one types of prayer, including simple prayer, sacramental prayer, prayer of the forsaken, prayer of relinquishment, covenant prayer and authoritative prayer. To impose some order on this profusion, Foster proposes a threefold model of inward, outward, and upward prayer (xii). His orientational model has since been adopted by psychologists Kevin Ladd and Bernard Spilka (378) to account for prayer's character as "self-examination" (inward prayer), "human-human connection" (outward prayer), and "human-divine relationship" (upward prayer).

3. This hymn is also the title hymn of *Standing in the Need of Prayer: A Celebration of Black Prayer*, a collection of hymns and photographs commissioned by the Schomburg Center for Research in Black Culture of the New York Public Library.

4. For an extended account of Burke's use of *prayer* as a key term, see my essay "Burkean Perspectives on Prayer."

5. Earlier versions of the "Serenity Prayer" date back to 1937.

6. The widespread appearance of the "Serenity Prayer" on samplers, bookmarks, and other objects presents a striking instance of prayer functioning quite literally as "equipment for living."

CHAPTER 2

1. Andrew M. Miller, in *From Delos to Delphi*, identifies Chryses's prayer as a form of the "cult" hymn—as opposed to a "rhapsodic" hymn of praise—and notes its three-part structure. So does Kevin Crotty in *The Poetics of Supplication*.

2. In *Prayer and Greek Religion*, Simon Pulleyn notes the dimension of reciprocity, or *charis*, in Greek prayer. In particular, Pulleyn elaborates on the range of past and future contexts in which the gods have acted in a quid pro quo relationship: "Give," a supplicant might pray, "because I have given/will give" or as a consequence of their nature: "Give because you have given."

3. In *The Rhetorical Imagination of Kenneth Burke*, Ross Wolin notes that Burke's emphasis on address is often missed by scholars who track his "new" rhetoric of identification and not his corresponding traditionalism.

4. Indirection in address is a concern of speech-act theory with respect to performatives. A *locutionary act* (what is said) is distinguishable from an *illocutionary act* (what is intended). Acts of address need not take explicit form as vocatives to function as address. See J. L. Austin's *How to Do Things with Words*.

5. Foucault references one cultic group in classical antiquity known as the "Therapeutae," who were devoted to healing, meditation, prayer, and other forms of self-care (21).

6. Foucault's characterization of the aims of technologies of the self, "to attain a certain state of happiness, purity, wisdom, perfection, or immortality" (18), is quite similar to Kenneth Burke's identification of prayer as a character-building discourse in *Attitudes Toward History*.

7. Christian practices of contemplation known as "centering prayer" owe their contemporary revival to Cistercian monks Thomas Keating and Basil Pennington. Pennington's *Centering Prayer* is a major source for devotional practice.

8. Rhetoric addressed directly or indirectly to the self as audience is a mode of argumentation Chaim Perelman and Lucie Olbrechts-Tyteca characterize in *The New Rhetoric* as "self-deliberation" (44). Jeanne Nienkamp addresses the broader category of such acts in *Internal Rhetorics*.

9. A wide range of texts fusing science with spirituality dates back to 1975 and Fritjof Capra's *The Tao of Physics*, a breakthrough text in popular metaphysics, and even further back to 1875 and Mary Baker Eddy's *Science and Health with Key to the Scriptures*, the foundational text of Christian Science.

10. In choosing *divine* as a generic term for prayer's objects of address, I recognize that no term can satisfactorily represent the otherworldly audiences figured in prayer.

11. Bakhtin defines *utterance* in "The Problem of Speech Genres" as the basic pragmatic unit of discourse marked by reciprocal turn taking.

12. Rayner draws on insights into the legitimating functions of audience/viewer in Lyotard's "Speech Snapshots."

13. The term *felicity conditions* is used in speech-act theory to describe elements of a discursive situation required for a successful outcome.

14. Kay Halasek argues that this "superaddressee rescues the utterance from the horrendous possibility of a 'lack of response'" (61, quoting Bakhtin, "Problem of the Text" 127).

CHAPTER 3

1. Among many contemporary texts that claim prayer in conversational terms are Don Aycock's *How to Have a Conversation with God*, Kyle Lake's *Reunderstanding Prayer*, and Lloyd Ogilvie's *Conversation with God*.

2. The *Rhetorica*'s characterization of apostrophe resembles that of *ecphonesis*, an exclamation expressing great emotion, in Richard Lanham's *Handlist of Rhetorical Terms*. Lanham

cross-references *ecphonesis* with *apostrophe*, offering examples from Henry Peacham's 1593 text *The Garden of Eloquence*: "O lamentable estate! O cursed misery! O rare and singular beauty!" (Peacham qtd. in Lanham 61).

CHAPTER 4

1. The character of prayerfulness is marked by some as a mode of awareness such that "each task we perform, from the most mundane upwards, becomes an occasion for prayerful listening and celebration" (Walters 97). It is a perspective on prayer as the "common business" of life particularly associated with the Carmelite monk Brother Lawrence (1614–91), whose posthumous *The Practice of the Presence of God* has attained the status of a spiritual classic in Catholic, Orthodox, and Protestant circles.

2. Responding to Saint Paul, theologian Paul Tillich recognizes a "paradox" in prayer being "humanly impossible" (135). The easier prayer becomes, whether because of spontaneity or liturgical fixity, the less authentic it will be.

3. See John Calvin's *The First Epistle of Paul the Apostle to the Corinthians*.

4. Here one thinks especially of a mime "acting out" an idea or emotion through the body as an expressive instrument.

5. See, for example, Celeste Snowber's *Embodied Prayer* and Jay Michaelson's *God in Your Body*, to cite but two among many recent works that emphasize the role of the body in prayer.

6. The (re)turn to the body in rhetorical studies was given a symbolic textual embodiment in Jack Selzer and Sharon Crowley, *Rhetorical Bodies*, an anthology of essays resulting from the 1997 Penn State Conference on Rhetoric and Composition focused on material rhetoric.

7. Debra Hawhee also notes Burke's ambivalence in the assignment of attitude, citing his insistence that "what we want is *not terms that avoid ambiguity*, but *terms that clearly reveal the strategic spots at which ambiguities necessarily arise*" (*GM* xvi, emphasis in original, qtd. in *Moving Bodies* 123).

8. In a recent online sermon, "Essential Attitudes of Effective Prayer," Richard O'Ffill's observations that "our characters are to a large extent the sum of our attitudes" and, a sentence later, that "it is a person's attitude that makes them do the things they do" nicely echo Burke's understanding of attitude as a productively indeterminate phenomenon of both agents and acts in *A Rhetoric of Motives*.

9. In her essay, "'The Piety of Degradation,'" Jordynn Jack productively demonstrates the degree to which Burke's concept of piety was shaped by his work in the 1920s on crime and drug addiction for the Bureau of Social Hygiene. Jack thus situates Burkean piety in both bodily and linguistic contexts.

10. A clear instance of pious attitudes as modes of incipient action are the "theological virtues" of faith, hope, and charity. Indeed, *virtues*, according to the *Catechism of the Catholic Church*, are "firm attitudes, stable dispositions, habitual perfections of intellect and will" (443). Both virtue and vice are attitudes.

11. For a substantive account of a theology of beauty anchored in the poetry of Hopkins, see Alejandro Garcia-Rivera's *The Community of Beauty*. For an engaging linguistic account of Hopkins's theological aesthetics, see Haj Ross Jr.'s "Beauty."

12. *Sprung rhythm* is a poetic meter in which "only accentual stresses count in the metrics of a line, and all poetic feet begin with a stressed syllable" (Vendler 9).

13. Kushner's "AIDS Prayer" was first delivered at the Episcopalian National Day of Prayer for AIDS on October 9, 1994, at the Cathedral of Saint John the Divine in New York City, later published as an excerpt in *Harper's*, and printed in full in Kushner's *Thinking About the Longstanding Problems of Virtue and Happiness*.

14. The notion of wrestling or contending with God has a narrative marker in the Genesis scene where Jacob wrestles through the night with someone who may be an angel of the Lord. The injured but unbowed Jacob is given a new name: "You shall no longer be called Jacob, but Israel, for you have striven with God and with humans, and have prevailed" (32:28).

15. Among the most penetrating accounts of prayer as a rhetoric of excess is Jean-Luc Marion's *In Excess*.

16. Stephen H. Webb discerns a linkage between hyperbolic excess and ethical responsibility in his insightful reading of Emmanuel Levinas on obligation: Levinas's "rhetoric as well as his method is hyperbolic precisely because he cannot philosophize as usual about the fundamental situation of being obligated" ("Rhetoric of Ethics" 4).

CHAPTER 5

1. More recently, Wills—a self-confessed amateur on Augustine—has written *Saint Augustine's Memory* (following *Saint Augustine's Childhood*), in which he explicates Augustine's intellectual and spiritual encounters with memory.

2. Frances Yates's seminal work *The Art of Memory* retrieved the vibrancy of the classical canon of memory for a modern era and spawned additional groundbreaking work in memory studies, including Mary Carruthers's *The Book of Memory* and *The Craft of Thought*.

3. In "Augustine's Philosophy of Memory," Roland Teske observes that the *Confessions* may be read as a work devoted to memory focused on past things (books 1–9), present things (book 10), and future things (books 11–13).

4. For a historical survey of the term *sensus communis* in rhetorical tradition, see John D. Schaeffer's essay "Sensus Communis." Schaeffer provides a more detailed account of the term in his earlier work, *Sensus Communis*.

5. The Memorare is an adaptation and excerpt from another Marian prayer, Ad sanctitatis tuae pedes, dulcissima Virgo Maria (At the Feet of Thy Holiness, Sweetest Virgin Mary), dating back to 1518. See Herbert Thurston's *Familiar Prayers*.

6. The Rosary is a devotion accomplished through the systematic recitation of multiple prayers and reflections, including the Pater Noster and the Ave Maria. For a brief history of this devotional practice, see Garry Will's *The Rosary*.

7. Recitation of the Memorare under proper conditions would grant a partial indulgence of three hundred days.

8. Although Vygotsky himself does not employ the term *activity system* in his writings on developmental psychology, rooted in observations of children at play (see especially *Mind in Society*), Vygotskian notions of activity form the basis for cultural-historical activity theory (CHAT), which does employ the term to describe the systemic use of artifacts by individuals within communities (see, for example, Engestrom, Miettien, and Punamaki).

CHAPTER 6

1. Ramie Targoff illuminates the dimensions of theatricality and the tropes of sincerity in this scene from *Hamlet* in *Common Prayer*.

2. My use of "vehicle" in this context is not intended to correspond to that of I. A. Richards in defining metaphor as a relationship between *tenor*, "the underlying idea or principle subject which the vehicle or figure means," and *vehicle*, "the saying we use to communicate that idea," in *The Philosophy of Rhetoric* (96–97). It is worth noting that Richards's model of metaphoricity is itself an instance of Reddy's "conduit metaphor."

3. In Catholic nomenclature, such objects are known as "sacramentals." Whereas sacraments, understood to be outward signs of grace, confer grace directly, sacramentals do so indirectly. In *Material Christianity*, Colleen McDannell underscores the importance of material objects and physical environments—as opposed to ideational concepts—to religious experience.

4. The distinction between icon and idol has much in common with Kenneth Burke's distinction between metonymy and synecdoche in "Four Master Tropes" (*GM* 508–9). The idol is a metonymic reduction, and the icon a representative synecdoche, of some reality.

5. In the nineteenth-century elocution movement, delivery became an adjunct of style when manner fused with mode. Stylistic qualities of clarity, forcefulness, and liveliness were thought to "naturally" correspond with speaking practices involving intonation, pacing, volume, and comportment of the body. Works such as John Bulwer's 1644 *Chirologia* and Gilbert Austin's 1806 *Chironomia* testify to the significance of the body and the voice as performative instruments in tandem.

6. A burgeoning scholarship has begun to document and theorize the migration of religion into cyberspace, including Stephen O'Leary's early "Cyberspace as Sacred Space," Brenda Brasher's *Give Me That Online Religion*, and collected works in Lorne Dawson and Douglas Cowan, eds., *Religion Online*.

7. The Church of England sponsored a similar effort in the 2009 Lenten season. In the 2011 Lenten season, the Say ONE for Me website clarified that each prayer or prayer request would be read and prayed over by one of several contemplative communities in addition to the Anglican bishops. Sometime after Lent 2011, however, Say ONE for Me was renamed "Pray ONE for Me" and converted to a year-round website (http://www.prayoneforme.org); while preserving the central feature of allowing visitors to submit their prayers or prayer requests and to have others pray for them, the website's home page was entirely redesigned.

8. In useful terms offered by Deborah Brandt, Say ONE for Me and similar websites function as "sponsors of literacy" when they recruit textual performance in the form of prayer.

9. Both delivery and reception may be understood as distributed activities, instances of what Prior and Shipka have characterized in terms of "chronotopic lamination."

Works Cited

Anderson, Dana. "Questioning the Motives of Habituated Action: Burke and Bourdieu on Practice." *Philosophy and Rhetoric* 37.3 (2004): 255–74.

Anonymous. "The Nine Ways of Prayer of St. Dominic." In *Early Dominicans: Selected Writings*, ed. Simon Tugwell, 94–103. Mahwah, NJ: Paulist Press, 1982.

Aristotle. *On Rhetoric: A Theory of Civic Discourse*. Trans. George Kennedy. Oxford: Oxford University Press, 1992.

Assmann, Jan. *Religion and Cultural Memory: Ten Studies*. Trans. Rodney Livingstone. Stanford: Stanford University Press, 2006.

Aycock, Don M. *How to Have a Conversation with God: Prayer That Draws Us Closer to the Father*. Grand Rapids: Kregel, 2004.

Augustine. *Confessions*. Trans. Henry Chadwick. Oxford: Oxford University Press, 1991.

Austin, Gilbert. *Chironomia: or A Treatise on Rhetorical Delivery*. Ed. Mary Margaret Robb and Lester Thonssen. 1806. Carbondale: Southern Illinois University Press, 1966.

Austin, J. L. *How to Do Things with Words*. Ed. J. O. Urmson and Marina Sbisa. 2nd ed. Cambridge, MA: Harvard University Press, 1962.

Bakhtin, M[ikhail] M[ikhailovich]. "Forms of Time and of the Chronotope in the Novel." In *The Dialogic Imagination: Four Essays*, ed. Michael Holquist, 84–258. Trans. Caryl Emerson and Michael Holquist. Austin: University of Texas Press, 1981.

———. "The Problem of Speech Genres." In *Speech Genres and Other Late Essays*, ed. Caryl Emerson and Michael Holquist, 60–102. Trans. Vern W. McGee. Austin: University of Texas Press, 1986.

———. "The Problem of the Text in Linguistics, Philology, and the Human Sciences: An Experiment in Philosophical Analysis." In *Speech Genres and Other Late Essays*, ed. Caryl Emerson and Michael Holquist, 103–31. Trans. Vern W. McGee. Austin: University of Texas Press, 1986.

———. "Toward Reworking the Dostoevsky Book." Appendix II. In *Problems of Dostoevsky's Poetics*, ed. and trans. Caryl Emerson, 283–304. Introd. Wayne C. Booth. Minneapolis: University of Minnesota Press, 1984.

Barth, Karl. *Prayer*. 1949. Trans. Sara F. Terrien. Ed. Don E. Saliers. With essays by Don E. Saliers, I. John Hesselink, Daniel L. Migliore, and Donald K. McKim. Louisville: Westminster John Knox Press, 2002.

Benson, Bruce Ellis, and Norman Wirzba. *The Phenomenology of Prayer*. New York: Fordham University Press, 2005.

Bitzer, Lloyd. "The Rhetorical Situation." *Philosophy and Rhetoric* 1.1 (1968): 1–14.

Boas, Frank. *Ethnology of the Kwakiutl*. In *Thirty-Fifth Annual Report of the Bureau of American Ethnology to the Secretary of the Smithsonian Institution, 1913–1914*. Part 1: pp. 48–794. Washington, DC: Government Printing Office, 1921.

Bolter, Jay David, and Richard Grusin. *Remediation: Understanding New Media*. Cambridge, MA: MIT Press, 2000.

Booth, Wayne C. *The Rhetoric of Rhetoric: The Quest for Effective Communication*. Oxford: Blackwell, 2004.

Bourdieu, Pierre. *The Logic of Practice*. Stanford: Stanford University Press, 1990.

Bourdieu, Pierre, and Loic J. D. Wacquant. "Interest, Habitus, Rationality." In *An Invitation to Reflexive Sociology*, ed. Pierre Bourdieu and Loic J. D. Wacquant, 115–39. Chicago: University of Chicago Press, 1992.

Brandt, Deborah. "Sponsors of Literacy." *College Composition and Communication* 49.2 (1998): 165–85.

Brasher, Brenda. *Give Me That Online Religion*. New Brunswick: Rutgers University Press, 2004.

Brinton, Alan. "Situation in the Theory of Rhetoric." *Philosophy and Rhetoric* 14.4 (1981): 234–48.

Brueggemann, Walter. *Awed to Heaven, Rooted in Earth: Prayers of Walter Brueggemann*. Ed. Walter Brueggemann and Edwin Searcy. Minneapolis: Augsburg Fortress, 2003.

———. *Great Prayers of the Old Testament*. Louisville: Westminster John Knox Press, 2008.

———. *The Psalms and the Life of Faith*. Minneapolis: Augsburg Fortress, 1995.

Buber, Martin. *I and Thou*. 1923. 2nd ed. Trans. Ronald Gregor Smith. New York: Scribner, 1984.

Bulwer, John. *Chirologia: or The Natural Language of the Hand* and *Chironomia: or The Art of Manual Rhetoric*. 1644. Ed. John Cleary. Carbondale: Southern Illinois University Press, 1974.

Burke, Kenneth. *Attitudes Toward History*. 3rd ed. Berkeley: University of California Press, 1984.

———. *A Grammar of Motives*. Berkeley: University of California Press, 1969.

———. *Language as Symbolic Action*. Berkeley: University of California Press, 1966.

———. *Permanence and Change*. 3rd ed. Berkeley: University of California Press, 1984.

———. *The Philosophy of Literary Form: Studies in Symbolic Action*. 3rd ed. Berkeley: University of California Press, 1984.

———. *A Rhetoric of Motives*. Berkeley: University of California Press, 1969.

———. *The Rhetoric of Religion: Studies in Logology*. 1961. Berkeley: University of California Press, 1970.

Calvin, John. *The First Epistle of Paul the Apostle to the Corinthians*. Trans. John W. Fraser. 1960. Vol. 9 of *Calvin's New Testament Commentaries*. Ed. David W. Torrance and Thomas F. Torrance. Grand Rapids: Eerdmans, 1996.

Campbell, Heidi. "Religion and the Internet." *Communication Research Trends* 25.1 (2006): 3–24.

Capra, Fritjof. *The Tao of Physics: An Exploration of the Parallels Between Modern Physics and Eastern Mysticism*. Boston: Shambhala, 1975.

Carruthers, Mary. *The Book of Memory: A Study in Medieval Culture*. Cambridge: Cambridge University Press, 1990.

———. *The Craft of Thought: Meditation, Rhetoric, and the Making of Images, 400–1200*. Cambridge: Cambridge University Press, 2000.

Catechism of the Catholic Church. Mahwah, NJ: Paulist Press, 1994.

Charney, Davida H. "Perfomativity and Persuasion in the Hebrew Book of Psalms: A Rhetorical Analysis of Psalms 116 and 22." *Rhetoric Society Quarterly* 40.3 (2010): 247–68.

Consigny, Scott. "Rhetoric and Its Situations." *Philosophy and Rhetoric* 7.3 (1974): 175–186.

Crotty, Kevin. *The Poetics of Supplication: Homer's "Iliad" and "Odyssey."* Ithaca: Cornell University Press, 2004.

Crowley, Sharon. *Toward a Civil Discourse: Rhetoric and Fundamentalism.* Pittsburgh: University of Pittsburgh Press, 2006.

Culler, Jonathan. *The Pursuit of Signs: Semiotics, Literature, Deconstruction.* Ithaca: Cornell University Press, 1981.

Cunningham, David. *Faithful Persuasion: In Aid of a Rhetoric of Christian Theology.* South Bend: University of Notre Dame Press, 1993.

Dawson, Lorne, and Douglas E. Cowan, eds. *Religion Online: Finding Faith on the Internet.* New York: Routledge, 2004.

Derrida, Jacques. "How to Avoid Speaking: Denials." In *Psyche: Inventions of the Other,* ed. Peggy Kamuf and Elizabeth Rottenberg, 2:143–95. 2 vols. Stanford: Stanford University Press, 2007.

Dhalla, M. M. "Homage unto Ahura Mazda." http://www.zarathushtra.com/z/article/dhalla/index.htm. Accessed 5 April 2012.

Dossey, Larry. *Healing Words: The Power of Prayer and the Practice of Medicine.* San Francisco: HarperCollins, 1993.

Durkheim, Emile. *The Elementary Forms of the Religious Life: A Study in Religious Sociology.* Trans. Carol Cosman. New York: Oxford University Press, 2008.

Dutton, Elisabeth. *Julian of Norwich: A Revelation of Love.* Lanham, MD: Rowman and Littlefield, 2008.

Eddy, Mary Baker. *Science and Health with Key to the Scriptures.* 1875. Boston: Christian Science Board of Directors, 1994.

Engestrom, Yrjo, Riejo Miettien, and Raija-Leena Punamaki. *Perspectives on Activity Theory.* Cambridge: Cambridge University Press, 1999.

Esslemont, J. E. *Bahá'u'lláh and the New Era.* 1937. 5th ed. Wilmette, IL: Bahá'í Publishing Trust, 1987.

FitzGerald, William T. "Burkean Perspectives on Prayer: Charting a Key Term Through Burke's Corpus." In *Kenneth Burke and His Circles,* ed. Jack Selzer and Robert Weiss, 201–21. West Lafayette, IN: Parlor Press, 2008.

Fontanier, Pierre. *Les figures du discours.* 1830. Paris: Flammarion, 1968.

Ford-Grabowsky, Mary. *Prayers for All People.* New York: Doubleday, 1995.

Foster, Richard J. *Prayer: Finding the Heart's True Home.* San Francisco: HarperCollins, 1992.

———. *Prayers from the Heart.* New York: HarperCollins, 1994.

Foucault, Michel. *Technologies of the Self: A Seminar with Michel Foucault.* Ed. Michel Foucault, Luther H. Martin, Huck Gutman, and Patrick H. Hutton. Amherst: University of Massachusetts Press, 1988.

Garcia-Rivera, Alejandro. *The Community of Beauty: A Theological Aesthetics.* Collegeville, MN: Liturgical Press, 1999.

George, Diana, and Mariolina Rizzi Salvatori. "Holy Cards/Immaginette: The Extraordinary Literacy of Vernacular Religion." *College Composition and Communication* 60.2 (2008): 250–84.

Giardini, Fabio. *Prayer Without Ceasing: Toward a Systematic Psychotheology of Christian Prayer.* Leominster, UK: Gracewing, 1998.

Griffin, Emilie. *Simple Ways to Pray: Spiritual Life in the Catholic Tradition.* Lanham, MD: Rowman and Littlefield, 2005.

Gschwandtner, Christina M. "Praise—Pure and Personal? Jean-Luc Marion's Phenom-enologies of Prayer." In *The Phenomenonology of Prayer*, ed. Bruce Ellis Benson and Norman Wirzba, 168–81. New York: Fordham University Press, 2005.

Halasek, Kay. *A Pedagogy of Possibility: Bakhtinian Perspectives on Composition Studies.* Carbondale: Southern Illinois University Press, 1999.

Hallesby, Ole. *Prayer.* Minneapolis: Augsburg Fortress, 1994.

Hardon, John A., S. J. "The Magnificat: Mary's Own Prayer." http://www.therealpresence. org/archives/Mariology/Mariology_017.htm. Accessed 10 November 2011.

Hawhee, Debra. *Bodily Arts: Rhetoric and Athletics in Ancient Greece.* Austin: University of Texas Press, 2004.

———. *Moving Bodies: Kenneth Burke at the Edges of Languages.* Columbia: University of South Carolina Press. 2009.

Helland, Christopher. "Surfing for Salvation." *Religion* 32.4 (2002): 293–302.

Hirshfield, Jane, ed. *Women in Praise of the Sacred: 43 Centuries of Spiritual Poetry by Women.* New York: HarperCollins, 1994.

Holquist, Michael. *Dialogism: Bakhtin and His World.* London: Routledge, 1990.

Homer. *The Iliad.* Trans. Richmond Lattimore. Chicago: University of Chicago Press, 1951.

———. *The Odyssey.* Trans. Robert Fitzgerald. New York: Random House, 1963.

Hopkins, Gerard Manley. "Pied Beauty." In *The Poems of Gerard Manley Hopkins*, ed. W. H. Gardner and N. H. MacKenzie, 69–70. 4th ed. Oxford: Oxford University Press, 1967.

Jack, Jordyn. "'The Piety of Degradation': Kenneth Burke, the Bureau of Social Hygiene, and *Permanence and Change.*" *Quarterly Journal of Speech* 90.4 (2004): 446–68.

James, William. *The Varieties of the Religious Experience.* 1902. New York: Penguin, 1982.

Jost, Walter, and Wendy Olmsted, eds. *A Companion to Rhetoric and Rhetorical Criticism.* Oxford: Blackwell, 2004.

———, eds. *Rhetorical Invention and Religious Inquiry: New Perspectives.* New Haven: Yale University Press, 2000.

Kierkegaard, Søren. *The Prayers of Kierkegaard.* Ed. Perry D. Lefevre. Chicago: University of Chicago Press, 1956.

———. *Purity of Heart Is to Will One Thing.* Trans. Douglas V. Steere. New York: Harper and Row, 1956.

Kushner, Tony. *Thinking About the Longstanding Problems of Virtue and Happiness: Essays, a Play, Two Poems, and a Prayer.* New York: Theater Communications Group, 1995.

Ladd, Kevin L., and Bernard Spilka. "Inward, Outward, Upward: Cognitive Aspects of Prayer." *Journal for the Scientific Study of Religion* 41.3 (2002): 375–84.

Lake, Kyle. *Reunderstanding Prayer: A Fresh Approach to Conversation with God.* Orlando, FL: Relevant Books, 2005.

Lanham, Richard. *A Handlist of Rhetorical Terms.* 2nd ed. Berkeley: University of California Press, 1991.

Lawrence, Brother. *The Practice of the Presence of God with Spiritual Maxims.* Grand Rapids: Spire Books, 2006.

Levinas, Emmanuel. "Prayer Without Demand." In *The Levinas Reader*, ed. Sean Hand, 227–34. Oxford: Blackwell, 1989.

———. *Totality and Infinity: An Essay on Exteriority.* Pittsburgh: Duquesne University Press, 1969.

Levine, Herbert J. *Sing unto God a New Song: A Contemporary Reading of the Psalms.* Bloomington: Indiana University Press, 1995.

Lewis, C. S. *Letters to Malcolm: Chiefly on Prayer.* New York: Harcourt, Brace and World, 1964.

Life Prayers: From Around the World, 365 Prayers, Blessings, and Affirmations to Celebrate the Human Journey. Ed. Elizabeth Roberts and Elias Amidon. New York: HarperCollins, 1996.

Linn, Jan. *Living Inside Out: Learning How to Pray the Serenity Prayer.* St. Louis: Chalice Press, 1994.

Lyotard, Jean-François. "Speech Snapshot." In *The Inhuman: Reflections on Time,* trans. Geoffrey Bennington and Rachel Bowlby, 129–34. Stanford: Stanford University Press, 1991.

Macquarrie, John. *Christian Hope.* New York: Seabury Press, 1978.

Marion, Jean-Luc. *God Without Being: Hors Texte.* Trans. Thomas A. Carlson. Chicago: University of Chicago Press, 1995.

———. *In Excess: Studies of Saturated Phenomena.* Trans. Robyn Horner and Vincent Berraud. New York: Fordham University Press, 2002.

Martin, Father James, S. J. *The Jesuit Guide to (Almost) Everything: A Spirituality for Real Life.* New York: HarperCollins, 2010.

McDannell. Colleen. *Material Christianity: Religion and Popular Culture in America.* New Haven: Yale University Press, 1995.

McKeon, Richard. "The Uses of Rhetoric in a Technological Age: Architectonic Productive Arts." In *Selected Writings of Richard McKeon.* Vol. 2, *Culture, Education, and the Arts,* ed. Richard Peter McKeon, Zahava Karl McKeon, and William G. Swenson, 197–216. Chicago: University of Chicago Press, 2005.

McLuhan, Marshall. *Understanding Media: The Extensions of Man.* 1964. Cambridge, MA: MIT Press, 1994.

Michaelson, Jay. *God in Your Body: Kabbalah, Mindfulness, and Embodied Spiritual Practice.* Woodstock: Jewish Lights, 2007.

Miller, Andrew M. *From Delos to Delphi: A Literary Study of the Homeric Hymn to Apollo.* Leiden: E. J. Brill, 1986.

Miller, Carolyn R. "Genre as Social Action." *Quarterly Journal of Speech* 70 (May 1984): 151–67.

Miller, J. Hillis. *For Derrida.* New York: Fordham University Press, 2009.

Milton, John. "Eikonoklastes." 1649. In *The Complete Prose Works of John Milton,* vol. 3, ed. Don M. Wolfe, 335–601. New Haven: Yale University Press, 1982.

Moore, James P. *Prayer in America: A Spiritual History of Our Nation.* New York: Doubleday, 2007.

Mountford, Roxanne. *The Gendered Pulpit: Preaching in American Protestant Spaces.* Carbondale: Southern Illinois University Press, 2005.

Nienkamp, Jean. *Internal Rhetorics: Toward a History and Theory of Self-Persuasion.* Carbondale: University of Southern Illinois Press, 2001.

O'Ffill, Richard. "Essential Attitudes of Effective Prayer." http://www.revivalsermons.org/sermons/essential_attitudes_effective_prayer.shtml. Accessed 23 January 2012.

Ogilvie, Lloyd John. *Conversation with God: Experience the Life-Changing Impact of Personal Prayer.* Eugene, OR: Harvest House, 1993.

O'Leary, Stephen D. "Cyberspace as Sacred Space: Communicating Religion on Computer Networks." *Journal of the American Academy of Religion* 64.4 (1996): 781–808.

Ong, Walter J., S. J. *The Presence of the Word: Some Prolegomena for Cultural and Religious History.* New Haven: Yale University Press, 1967.

———. *Orality and Literacy: The Technologizing of the Word.* London: Routledge, 2004.

Orsi, Robert A. "The Center Out There, In Here, and Everywhere Else: The Nature of Pilgrimage to the Chicago Shrine of Saint Jude, 1929–1965." *Journal of Social History* 25.2 (1991): 213–32.

———. *Thank You, St. Jude: Women's Devotion to the Patron Saint of Hopeless Causes.* New Haven: Yale University Press, 1998.

Pennington, Basil. *Centering Prayer: Renewing an Ancient Christian Prayer Form.* New York: Doubleday, 1982.

Perelman, Chaim, and Lucie Olbrechts-Tyteca. *The New Rhetoric: A Treatise on Argumentation.* South Bend: University of Notre Dame Press, 1969.

Prior, Paul, and Jody Shipka. "Chronotopic Lamination: Tracing the Contours of Literate Activity." In *Writing Selves, Writing Societies: Research from Activity Perspectives,* ed. Charles Bazerman and David Russell, 180–238. Fort Collins, CO: WAC Clearinghouse and Mind, Culture, and Activity, 2003. http://wac.colostate.edu/books/selves_societies/. Accessed 23 January 2012.

Pulleyn, Simon. *Prayer in Greek Religion.* Oxford: Oxford University Press, 1997.

Raccolta: or Collection of Indulgenced Prayers. Trans. Fr. Ambrose St. John. 1866. http://www.archive.org/details/raccoltaorcolleoostjgoog. Accessed 23 January 2012.

Rahner, Karl. *The Need and Blessing of Prayer.* 3rd ed. Trans. Bruce Gillette. Collegeville, MN: Liturgical Press, 1997.

Ratcliffe, Krista. *Rhetorical Listening: Identification, Gender, Whiteness.* Carbondale: Southern Illinois University Press, 2005.

Rayner, Alice. "The Audience: Subjectivity, Community, and the Ethics of Listening." *Journal of Dramatic Theory and Criticism* 8:2 (2003): 1–21.

Reddy, Michael J. "The Conduit Metaphor: A Case of Frame Conflict in Our Language About Language." In *Metaphor and Thought,* ed. Andrew Ortony, 164–201. 2nd ed. Cambridge: Cambridge University Press, 1993.

Rhetorica ad Herennium. By [Cicero]. Trans. Harry Caplan. Loeb Classical Library. Cambridge, MA: Harvard University Press, 1954.

Richards, I. A. *The Philosophy of Rhetoric.* Oxford: Oxford University Press, 1965.

Ross, Haj, Jr. "Beauty: How Hopkins Pied It." *Language Sciences* 21.3 (1999): 237–50.

Russell, David. "Rethinking Genre in School and Society: An Activity Theory Analysis." *Written Communication* 14.4 (1997): 504–54.

Santayana, George. *The Life of Reason: or The Phases of Human Progress.* Vol. 1. New York: Scribner, 1905.

Schaeffer, John D. "Sensus Communis." In *A Companion to Rhetoric and Rhetorical Criticism,* ed. Walter Jost and Wendy Olmsted, 278–93. Oxford: Blackwell, 2004.

———. *Sensus Communis: Vico, Rhetoric, and the Limits of Relativism.* Chapel Hill: Duke University Press, 1990.

Schomburg Center for Research in Black Culture. *Standing in the Need of Prayer: A Celebration of Black Prayer.* New York: Free Press, 2003.

Selzer, Jack, and Sharon Crowley, eds. *Rhetorical Bodies.* Madison: University of Wisconsin Press, 1999.

Shakespeare, William. *Hamlet.* In *The Riverside Shakespeare*, 1183–1245. 2nd ed. Boston: Houghton Mifflin, 1997

Sifton, Elizabeth. *The Serenity Prayer: Faith and Politics in Times of Peace and War.* New York: Norton, 2001.

Sipiora, Phillip. "Introduction: The Ancient Concept of *Kairos*." In *Rhetoric and Kairos: Essays in History, Theory, and Praxis*, ed. Phillip Sipiora and James S. Baumlin, 1–22. Albany: State University of New York Press, 2002.

Smith, Jonathan Z. "Here, There, and Everywhere." In *Prayer, Magic, and the Stars in the Ancient and Late Antique World*, ed. Scott Noegel, Joel Thomas Walker, and Brannon M. Wheeler, 21–36. University Park: Pennsylvania State University Press, 2003.

Starhawk [Miriam Simos]. *The Spiral Dance: A Rebirth of the Ancient Religion of the Great Goddess.* New York: HarperCollins, 1999.

Struever, Nancy. *Rhetoric, Modality, Modernity.* Chicago: University of Chicago Press, 2009.

Sullivan, Dale. "Kairos and the Rhetoric of Belief." *Quarterly Journal of Speech* 78 (1992): 317–32.

Sweetser, Eve. *From Etymology to Pragmatics: Metaphorical and Cultural Aspects of Semantic Structure.* Cambridge: Cambridge University Press, 1990.

Targoff, Ramie. *Common Prayer: The Language of Public Devotion in Early Modern England.* Chicago: University of Chicago Press, 2001.

Teilhard de Chardin, Pierre. *Hymn of the Universe.* New York: Harper and Row, 1965.

Tell, David. "Burke's Encounter with Ransom: Rhetoric and Epistemology in 'Four Master Tropes.'" *Rhetoric Society Quarterly* 34.4 (2004): 33–54.

Teresa of Avila. *Interior Castle.* Trans. E. Allison Peers. Radford, VA: Wilder, 2008.

———. *The Way of Perfection.* Trans. Henry L. Carrigan. London: Baronius Press, 2006.

Teske, Roland. "Augustine's Philosophy of Memory." In *The Cambridge Companion to Augustine*, ed. Eleanor Stump and Norman Kretzmann, 148–58. New York: Cambridge University Press, 2001.

Thurston, Herbert, S. J. *Familiar Prayers: Their Origin and History.* London: Burns and Oates, 1953.

Tillich, Paul. *The New Being.* Introd. Mary Ann Stenger. Lincoln: University of Nebraska Press, 2005.

Vatz, Richard E. "The Myth of the Rhetorical Situation." *Philosophy and Rhetoric* 6.3 (1973): 154–61.

Vendler, Helen. *The Breaking of Style: Hopkins, Heaney, Graham.* Cambridge, MA: Harvard University Press, 1995.

Voloshinov, Valentin. *Marxism and the Philosophy of Language.* Trans. Ladislav Matejka and I. R. Titunik. New York: Seminar Press, 1973.

Vygotsky, L. S. *Mind in Society: The Development of Higher Psychological Processes.* Cambridge, MA: Harvard University Press, 1978.

Walters, Kerry. *Spirituality of the Handmaid: A Model for Contemporary Seekers.* Mahwah, NJ: Paulist Press, 1999.

Webb, Stephen H. *Blessed Excess: Religion and the Hyperbolic Imagination.* Albany: State University of New York Press, 1993.

———. *Re-figuring Theology. The Rhetoric of Karl Barth.* Albany: State University of New York Press, 1991.

———. "The Rhetoric of Ethics as Excess: A Christian Theological Response to Emmanuel Levinas." *Modern Theology* 15.1 (1999): 1–16.

Wenger, Etienne. "Communities of Practice: A Brief Introduction." http://www.ewenger
.com/theory/. Accessed 10 October 2011.

Wilkinson, Bruce H. *The Prayer of Jabez: Breaking Through to the Blessed Life*. Sisters, OR:
Multnomah Press, 2000.

Wills, Garry. *The Rosary*. New York: Viking, 2005.

———. *Saint Augustine's Childhood*. New York: Viking, 2001.

———. *Saint Augustine's Memory*. New York: Viking, 2002.

Wirzba, Norman. "Attention and Responsibility: The Work of Prayer." In *The Phenomenology of Prayer*, ed. Bruce Ellis Benson and Norman Wirzba, 88–100. New York:
Fordham University Press, 2005.

Wolin, Ross. *The Rhetorical Imagination of Kenneth Burke*. Columbia: University of South
Carolina Press, 2001.

Wordsworth, William. "Preface to Lyrical Ballads." In William Wordsworth and Samuel
Taylor Coleridge, *Lyrical Ballads and Other Poems*, introd. and ed. Martin Scofield,
5–25. Wordsworth Poetry Library. Hertfordshire: Wordsworth Editions, 2003.

Yates, Frances A. *The Art of Memory*. Rev. ed. Chicago: University of Chicago Press, 2001.

Index

Abel, sacrifice of, 4–5
acceptance, frames of, 80
accuracy, 26–27
activity systems, 108–9, 142n8
address, markers of, 57. *See also* scene of address, prayer as
addressees, as audience, 44–45, 48
addressivity, 46
adoration, 83–84. *See also* praise
aesthetic, separation of ethical and, 65, 67
Agamemnon, 31–32
agency
    attitude and, 73, 79–80
    delivery and, 119
    Dossey on, 37–38
"AIDS Prayer" (Kushner), 85–86
aliens, 44
Anderson, Dana, 80
animals
    interaction with, 42
    as sacrifice, 4–5
anthropomorphism, 38
Apollo, Chryses's prayer to, 31–33, 40, 48–49, 50
apostrophe, invocation and, 61–64, 135
Aristotle, 16
artistic praise, 88
Assmann, Jan, 101
attention, and prayer as rehearsal, 21–24
attitude. *See also* reverence; sincerity
    Burke on, 141nn7–8
    coaching and dancing of, 74–83
    importance of, 74–75
    motive of, 7
    praise and, 83–91
    prayer as performance of, 4–5, 71–74, 135–36
    virtues and vices as, 141n10
audience
    addressees as, 44–45, 48
    divine beings as, 42

as element of situations, 14
and prayer as address, 40–41
rhetorical listening and, 47
Augustine, Saint, 103

Bakhtin, Mikhail
    on addressivity, 46
    concept of chronotope, 107
    on superaddressee, 49–50
    on utterance, 35, 61
Barth, Karl, 75
bedtime prayer, 18–19
being heard, hearing and, 46–51
Bernard, Claude, 104–5
Bernard of Clairvaux, 104
biblically based views, 37
Bitzer, Lloyd, 14–15
blessings, 1–2, 15–16
Boas, Franz, 92, 93
body
    delivery and, 121
    as expression of attitude, 76–79
    as instrument of performance, 35
    memory and, 112–13
Bolter, Jay David, 121–22, 129
Book of Common Prayer, 111
Booth, Wayne, 47
Bourdieu, Pierre, 80–81, 112
Brinton, Alan, 14
Brueggemann, Walter
    on lament, 86
    on orientation, 82
    on prayer as dangerous act, 52, 53
    on Psalm 30, 56
Buber, Martin, 60–61
Burke, Kenneth
    on accuracy of prayer, 26
    on acts and agents, 31
    on attitude, 73–74, 79–80, 89, 141nn7–8
    on communicating with divine, 45
    on dance of words and bodies, 71

Burke, Kenneth (*continued*)
  "Dialectician's Hymn," 26–30
  on magic, 38–39, 52, 53
  on mystery, 97–98
  on piety, 72, 141n9
  on prayer, 3, 22–23
  on pure persuasion, 60, 88, 129
  on rhetoric, 2–3, 45
  on scene-act and scene-agent relations, 54
  on secular prayer, 75–77, 81
  on situations, 16
  theory of dramatism, 6–7, 133
burning bush, 71

Cain, sacrifice of, 4–5
call to prayer, 13–14, 29
candles, 35, 127–28
Canticle of Mary, 90–91
Carruthers, Mary, 109, 110, 113
Catholic Mass, 102
centering prayer, 34, 140n7
character
  invocation and, 53
  shaping, as purpose of prayer, 23–24
Charney, Davida, 17
chronotope, 107
chronotopic lamination, 107
Chryses, prayer of, 31–33, 40, 48–49, 50
Church of England, 123, 143n7
Claudius, prayer of, 115–16
coaching of attitude, 76–83
"coffee prayer," 56–57
collective memory, 101
communicative memory, 101
community of practice, 109
conduit metaphor, 116
Confessions (Augustine), 103
Consigny, Scott, 14
constraints, as element of situations, 14
consubstantiality, linguistic, 43–44, 134
craft, prayer as socialized, 101
Creation, 87–88
Crotty, Kevin, 32
Culler, Jonathan, 62, 63, 64
cultural-historical activity theory (CHAT),
  108–9, 142n8
cultural memory, 101, 111
cyberprayer, 122–29, 131, 137
cyberworship, 122, 129

dance, attitude as, 76–83

deliberative discourse, 16–17
delivery
  in digital age, 121–30
  modes of, 118–21
  overview of, 115–18, 137
demons, 44
Derrida, Jacques, 65–66, 67
desire, as "aboutness" of prayer, 103–4
despair, 15
"Dialectician's Hymn" (Burke), 26–30
digital media, 120, 121–29, 137
divine beings
  naming, 67–70
  presence of, 52
  realm of, 41–46
divine names, 66, 67–70
Dominic, Saint, 78
Dossey, Larry, 36–39
dramatism, 6–7, 73, 79–80

Earth, 70
epideictic discourse, 16–17
"eternal Thou," 60–61
ethical, separation of aesthetic and, 65, 67
Eucharistic Prayer, 102
exigence, 13–15

felicity conditions, 48, 140n13
Fontanier, Pierre, 62–63
forensic discourse, 16–17
formality of address, 57, 58
Foster, Richard, 56–57, 83, 139n2
Foucault, Michel, 33, 140nn5–6
frames of acceptance, 80
frames of rejection, 80
Francis of Assisi, Saint, 104

genre, 20
God
  as "eternal Thou," 60–61
  law of, 102–3
Goddess movement, 69
greeting cards, 100
Grusin, Richard, 121–22, 129
Gschwandtner, Christina M., 66, 67

habitus, 80–81, 112–13
Halasek, Kay, 140n13
Hallesby, Ole, 73
Hamlet, 115–18
Hawhee, Debra, 15, 98, 112

Healing Words (Dossey), 36–39
health, prayer's effect on, 36
heard, hearing and being, 46–51
hearing, and being heard, 46–51
Helland, Christopher, 122
Heschel, Rabbi Abraham, 115
Holquist, Michael, 47–48
holy ground, 71–72
hope, prayer as instrument of, 28
Hopkins, Gerard Manley, 84–85
Hunt, George, 92
"Hymn to Matter" (Teilhard de Chardin),
    59–60
hyperbole, 89
hypermediacy, 129
hypocritical prayer, 121, 130
hypomnesis, 32

icons, 117–18
identity, 97–98
idols, 117–18
"I-It" relationship, 60–61
Iliad, 31–33, 40, 48–49, 50
illocutionary act, 56, 140n4
immediacy, hypermediacy and, 129
impiety, 71–72, 80
intercessory prayer, 124–28
Internet, 122–29, 131, 137
inventio, 110
invitation to prayer, 13–14, 29
invocation
    apostrophe and, 61–64
    dangers of, 135
    language of, 54–61
    naming divine and, 67–70
    overview of, 52–54
    phenomenology of, 64–67
    reverence and, 81
irreverence, 95
Israel, covenant with, 102–3
"I-Thou" relationship, 60–61

Jabez, 1
Jack, Jordynn, 141n9
James, William, 3
Jesus
    hypocritical prayer and, 121
    prayer to, 56–57
    Via Crucis and, 110–11
Jost, Walter, 3
Jude, Saint, 119, 126

judgment. *See* krisis
Julian of Norwich, 77

kairos, 13–18, 27, 28, 30
Keating, Thomas, 140n7
Kierkegaard, Søren, 52, 58–59
krisis, 13–18, 30
Kushner, Tony, 85–86
Kwakiutl, 92–95, 96

lament, 85–86
lamination, chronotopic, 107
language
    attitude and, 74–75
    of divine beings, 43–44
    of invocation, 54–61
    as motive of relationship, 46
    praise and, 85
    secular prayer and, 76
    transcending, 6
Lanham, Richard, 140–41n2
Lave, Jean, 109
Law of God, 102–3
Lawrence, Brother, 141n1
Levinas, Emmanuel, 3, 64–65, 67
Lewis, C. S., 1, 31
linguistic consubstantiality, 43–44, 134
listening, prayer as act of, 34
listening rhetoric, 47
literature, social functions of, 22–23
liturgical prayer, 102
living
    prayer as rehearsal for, 21–24, 133
    "Serenity Prayer" and rehearsal for, 24–28
location, 118–21
locutionary act, 140n4
love, mystery and, 97, 98
Lyotard, François, 47

machina memorialis, 110, 113
Macquarrie, John, 71
magic
    Burke on, 52
    invocation and, 53
    rhetoric and, 38–39
Magnificat, 90–91
Marion, Jean-Luc, 66–67, 117–18
markers of address, 57
Mary, 90–91, 104–7, 112
Mass, 102
Memorare, 104–9, 112

memoria, 110
memory
    as "aboutness" of prayer, 102–4
    devotional practices and, 110–12
    habitus and, 112–13
    Memorare and, 104–9
    and modality in prayer, 109–10
    prayer as rhetorical art of, 100–102, 113–14,
        136–37
metonymy, 27, 143n4
Miller, Andrew M., 32
Miller, Carolyn, 20
Miller, J. Hillis, 65–66
Milton, John, 111
mimesis, 76–79
modality, 109
"Modi orandi Sancti Dominici," 78
monsters, 44
Moses, 71–72
motives, in Burke's theory of dramatism, 6–7,
    73, 133
movement, prayer as, 115–18. *See also* delivery
mystery, 97–98

names and naming, 53, 66, 67–70
National Shrine to Saint Jude, 119, 126
nature, praise of, 87–88
Niebuhr, Reinhold, 25
"Nine Ways of Prayer of Saint Dominic, The,"
    78

obedience, 48
O'Ffill, Richard, 141n8
Olmsted, Wendy, 3
Ong, Walter, 47, 48, 120
online prayer, 122–29, 131, 137
online religion, 122
opportunity. *See* kairos
orans posture, 78–79
orientation, principle of, 82
Orsi, Robert, 119
other
    divine beings as, 43
    invocation of, 64, 65–66
otherworldly beings, 44. *See also* divine
    beings

Paisley, Ian, 71, 72, 95
Paul, Saint, 21, 74
Pennington, Basil, 140n7
Pernot, Laurent, 3

personification, prayer as, 38
persuasion
    mystery and identity and, 97–98
    pure, 60, 88, 129
petition, 19, 86
physical health, prayer's effect on, 36
"Pied Beauty" (Manley), 84–85
piety
    Burke on, 80, 141n9
    memory and, 112
    of Moses, 71–72
    in sacrifice and prayer, 4–5
plants, discourse with, 42–43
posture, 76–79, 112–13
practice, prayer as, 21–24
praise, 19, 83–91
prayer cards, 105
Prayer of Jabez, The (Wilkinson), 1–2
"Prayer of Saint Francis," 104
"Prayer to the Sockeye Salmon," 92–93
presence, through invocation, 52, 58, 60
principle of orientation, 82
Prior, Paul, 107
privacy, in prayer, 121
prophetic discourse, prayer as, 69
proverbs, 22
Psalm 148, 87–88
Psalm 30, 55–56
psalms, 17, 54, 55–56, 87–88
Pulleyn, Simon, 140n2
pure persuasion, 60, 88, 129
purpose, motive of, 7

Rahner, Karl, 15–16
Ratcliffe, Krista, 47
Rayner, Alice, 47, 48
recognition, and prayer as address, 40
Reddy, Michael, 116
rehearsal for living
    prayer as, 21–24, 133
    "Serenity Prayer" and, 24–28
rejection, frames of, 80
religion
    memory and, 101
    rhetoric and, 2–3
religion online, 122
remediation, 121–22
responsibility, and prayer as rehearsal, 21–24
reverence. *See also* attitude
    defined, 81–82
    forms of, 82–83

impulse toward, 91–95
objects and endurance of, 95–99
praise and, 83–91
prayer as performance of, 71–74, 135
in sacrifice and prayer, 4–5
rhetoric
Burke on, 45
magic and, 38–39
relationship between prayer and, 5–6
religion and, 2–3
rhetorical listening, 47

sacramentals, 117, 143n3
sacrifice, animal, 4–5
St Bernard Abbey's Online Chapel, 127–28
salmon, 92–95, 96
Santayana, George, 100
Say ONE for Me website, 123–26, 143n7
scene of address, prayer as
Chryses's prayer and, 31–33
conceptual and verbal, 40–41
Derrida on, 65
divine beings and, 41–46
Healing Words and, 36–39
hearing and being heard and, 46–51
overview of, 33–35
secular forms of address, 42
secular prayer, 23, 75–77, 81
sensus communis, 103–4
"Serenity Prayer," 24–28
set forms of prayer, 111–12
Shakespeare, William, 115
Shema, 48
Shipka, Jody, 107
Sifton, Elizabeth, 25
silence, 34
Simos, Miriam, 69
sincerity, 115–16, 130. *See also* attitude
Sipiora, Phillip, 15
situation(s)
numbering, 28–30
performative space and, 18–20
and prayer as address, 40
prayer as art of, 11–13, 133
and prayer as rehearsal, 21–24
of "Serenity Prayer," 24–28
space and time in rhetorical construction of, 13–18
Smith, Jonathan Z., 118–19, 129
sociality
prayer and, 109

reverence and, 91–92, 97–98
socialized craft, prayer as, 101
Sockeye salmon, 92–95, 96
space
Memorare and, 107
and prayer as rehearsal, 21–24
in rhetorical construction of situations, 13–18
scene of address as conceptual and performative, 41
"Serenity Prayer" and, 24–28
situation and performative, 18–20
sprung rhythm, 84, 141n12
"Standing in the Need of Prayer," 19–20
Starhawk, 69
Struever, Nancy, 11
Sullivan, Dale, 15
superaddressee, 49–50
Sweetser, Eve, 48
synecdoche, 27, 143n4

"technologies of the self," 33–34
technology, 120, 122–29, 131, 137
Teilhard de Chardin, Pierre, 59–60
Tell, David, 27
Teresa of Avila, 24
text, Memorare and modality of, 109
textual treasuries, 111
thanksgiving, prayers of, 19
theology, comparing prayer to, 12
Therapeutae, 140n5
Thurston, Herbert, 104
Tillich, Paul, 141n2
time
Memorare and, 107
and prayer as rehearsal, 22–24
in rhetorical construction of situations, 13–18
tradition, 69, 103–4, 107
treasuries, textual, 111
typologies, of prayer, 17

unceasing prayer, 21–22
utterance, 35, 46, 61

Vatz, Richard, 14
Via Crucis, 110–11
vices, 141n10
virtues, 141n10
Voloshinov, Valentin, 50–51
Vygotsky, Lev, 108–9, 142n8

Way of the Cross, 110–11
Webb, Stephen H., 89
websites, 122–29, 131, 137
Wenger, Etienne, 109
Wilkinson, Bruce, 1–2
Wills, Garry, 103
Wirzba, Norman, 12, 15, 21

Wolin, Ross, 140n3
Wordsworth, William, 91
work, 138
Wright, John, 21
"writing as going," 119

Zoroastrian hymn, 54–55